William Bodham Donne

Essays on the Drama and on Popular Amusements

William Bodham Donne

Essays on the Drama and on Popular Amusements

ISBN/EAN: 9783744697941

Printed in Europe, USA, Canada, Australia, Japan

Cover: Foto ©Thomas Meinert / pixelio.de

More available books at **www.hansebooks.com**

ESSAYS ON THE DRAMA,

AND

ON POPULAR AMUSEMENTS.

BY

WILLIAM BODHAM DONNE,

EXAMINER OF STAGE PLAYS, LORD CHAMBERLAIN'S OFFICE.

Reprinted from THE QUARTERLY REVIEW, THE WESTMINSTER
REVIEW, AND FRAZER'S MAGAZINE.

—————

SECOND EDITION.

LONDON:
TINSLEY, BROTHERS, CATHERINE STREET, STRAND,
AND
J. E. JONES, 12, EVERSHOLT STREET, N.W.
——
1863.

CONTENTS.

———◆———

ESSAYS ON THE DRAMA.

ATHENIAN COMEDY.*

M. Guizot's Essay upon the 'Life, Writings, and Age of Menander,' belongs to that order of 'studies' of classical antiquity in which Germany and France abound, but which are in little esteem at our own Universities. To this department the contributions of English scholars are few in number and inconsiderable in value. They have generally preferred the practical but somewhat dreary paths of pure philology, and left to foreigners the more attractive regions of biography and general criticism. Our periodical Journals occasionally present the reader with some excellent essays on ancient authors; but such lively and learned treatises as M. Guizot's are seldom, if ever, published under the auspices of the Pitt or the Clarendon press. We do not imagine our Bachelors and

---

* Reprinted from the 'Westminster Review.'

Ménandre; Etude Historique et Littéraire sur la Comédie et la Société Grecques. Par Guillaume Guizot. 8vo. Paris, 1855.

B

Masters of Arts to be less sensible than Continental scholars of the beauties of Classical Literature; but either they lack encouragement from the public, or are earlier engrossed by the cares of the world.

While the tragic drama and the Aristophanic comedy of the Athenians have attracted their due share of notice, both from those who amended their text, and those who entered into their dramatic or philosophical spirit, the new, or, as we may venture to phrase it, the Genteel Comedy of Athens, has elicited comparatively little attention. This partial neglect may be ascribed to two causes,—to the fragmentary condition in which the latest offspring of the Attic theatre has come down to us; and to the grander forms of imagination and art embodied in the elder drama. Through every disguise, through the change of creeds and ethical ideas, through the resisting medium of a dead language, through mutilation of parts and corruption of texts, through the mists of an extinct religion, and the veils of obsolete party feuds, the presence as of a great spirit standing before us is perceptible in the Athenian drama. Never was the indestructible life of Grecian genius more apparent than when, some years ago, Mendelssohn's 'Antigone' was produced on the London stage. The music alone was worthy of the story: the *libretto* was alternately tumid and feeble in its language; the actors were encumbered by the stilted sentiments put into their mouths, and baffled by the slow and sculpturesque evolutions and situations of the plot; the choruses looked and sang like Minor Canons gone distracted; and the costume bore about as close a resemblance to the original theatrical garb as the Eglinton tournament bore to the lists of Ashby. Yet, through every disadvantage and deformity, Mendelssohn's music was not the only impressive portion of the performance. If it did not transport the spectator to "Athens or Thebes," it brought him at least within ken of an august Titanic power from whose countenance not even the decay and dishonours of the grave had effaced all its primal beauty. For from beyond the tomb, and from a distant shore, and through the glare and dissonance of a modern theatre, came authentic voices of passion, and gleams of grandeur and loveliness, that rolled back the mists of centuries, and revealed at least a portion of the original brightness. Uncrowned and deposed, the majesty of Sophocles was still right royal, and asserted its claim to the homage of the spectators.

The Aristophanic comedy has never been put to a similar trial; and, even with the aid of music, could hardly be rendered intelligible to a modern audience. The ethical principles of Tragedy are the property of mankind: they rest upon our fontal passions; they resolve themselves into extant results. If "the woes of old great houses" formed the staple of so many Athenian dramas, they have also furnished the plots of 'Lear' and 'Hamlet'; if fights fought long ago were rehearsed by the author of the 'Seven against Thebes'

and the 'Phœnissæ,' the wars of the Roses and the
Barons no less filled the historical canvas of Shakespeare.   The Nemesis in 'Macbeth' is not less appalling than the Nemesis of the 'Œdipus;' and the vati-
cinations of Margaret of Anjou "strike as cold" as
those of Cassandra of Troy.   But Comedy enjoys no
similar privileges.   Its life is the life of the present;
it catches the Cynthia of the minute; its mirror,
unlike Agrippa's, reflects only the spirit of its own
age.   The Lord Burleigh of 'The Critic' is a pleasant burlesque; but the historical Lord Burleigh is
inadmissible in comedy.   An Athenian playwright
would have revelled in impersonations of Chatham's
gout and flannels; of Pitt's crane's-neck; of Sheridan's ruby nose, and Fox's shrill tones and bushy
eyebrows.   The modern dramatist who should reproduce them, would not cause even the injudicious
to laugh, and would be rewarded for his attempt by
a general sibilation.   We leave to Gilray and Leech
this department of the "comic business" of politics;
and, although our pantomimes occasionally indulge
in allusions to the Commissioners of Sewers and
Sabbath-Observance Bills, such matters are excluded
from comedy and even from farce.   Such was not the
usage of "Eupolis, Cratinus, and Aristophanes;" nor
did either the Government of the day or the public
demand from them any such abstinence.   The news
of the moment was mostly the theme of their dramas;
and the poet of the Old Comedy who should have

preferred general to local and contemporaneous topics
would as certainly have been hooted from the stage,
as a dramatic author would now be, if he brought
before the public the Convocation of the Clergy, or
committed a breach of privilege by parodying a
Maynooth debate. 'The Clouds' or 'The Birds'
would consequently not affect a modern audience
like the 'Medea' or the 'Antigone.' The satire
would be pointless; the allusions unintelligible;
the choral songs, in immediate connection with the
broadest farce, would seem to us a Mezentian union.
We should desire to consign the one to Grisi and
Mario, and banish the other to some suburban saloon.
The Aristophanic Comedy cannot be transplanted from
Greece at all, and hardly from the precincts of Athens.
The poet and his audience were nearly as local as
many of the interludes of Molière, expressly composed
for an occasional *fête* at Versailles. It is difficult to
conceive an audience more thoroughly absorbed in
the business of the scene, or less disposed to be easily
pleased, than an Athenian audience in the time of
Aristophanes. Usually it is sufficient to secure the
applause of spectators, if the plot of a comedy be
skilfully contrived, the manners faithfully copied from
the life, the morals at least conventionally sound,
the dilemma probable, the passions intelligibly evoked
and directed, and the humour and situations strange
or absurd enough for surprise and laughter. But
these conditions of success are as far from exhausting

the powers of Aristophanes, as they would have been
from contenting his susceptible and critical countrymen. It was not enough for the author of a popular
comedy to be a wit of the first order; he was required,
in the Old Comedy at least, to be a poet also of the
first rank. The songs of 'The Birds' and the choruses
of 'The Clouds' were not less essential to his "first
night," than the fun of Trygæus and Strepsiades.
We know not indeed whether the comic, like the
tragic dramatist, were necessarily a musician and a
ballet-master; but he certainly must have possessed,
in no ordinary measure, the gift of suiting his words
to the music and his situations to the dance; and we
can hardly conceive Aristophanes to have entrusted
any leader of the orchestra, or the professional Vestris
and D'Egville of his days, with either his complicate
songs or his grotesque ballets. Neither was it enough
for him to be a perfect master of his own art and its
scenic or pantomimical accompaniments. He must
have felt, or affected to feel, an intense interest in
whatsoever interested his countrymen at the moment,
whether it were the war in Sicily, the most recent
play by Euripides, or the last frolic of Alcibiades.
That Aristophanes himself was an active party-man
we know. He was a zealous member of the Peace
Society, and a hearty opponent of Young Athens and
the philosophers. Under the *régime* of the Old Comedy, indeed, the dramatic poet was not only author,
manager, musician, ballet-master, and perhaps actor

also, but he was the Athenian 'Times' and 'Punch;'
wielding alike the scourge of invective and ridicule, as
regarded politics, and the Athenian 'Quarterly' and
'Edinburgh,'—the Minos and Rhadamanthus of current literature.

And as was the poet, so was his audience. The
Athenians were essentially a dramatic people: sudden
and quick in their emotions, gifted with a keen perception of the beautiful and the ludicrous, with fine
organs of sense, and surrounded by objects the best
calculated to train, sharpen, and mature them. They
were moreover a gossiping, scurrilous, and news-
loving race, delighting in novelty, and impatient of
uniformity either in their business or amusements.
But predisposed as they were, in virtue of these qualities, to dramatic entertainments, they enjoyed only
brief opportunities (at least, so long as they adhered
to their old customs) of indulging this taste. Their
theatres were not open all the year round. Their
Opera-house—the Odeum—was closed after a brief
season; and their Theatre Royal—the Temple of
Bacchus—was licensed only during the greater and
the lesser Dionysiac Festivals,—that is, during a few
weeks in the spring of each year. Neither, as in
Rome, were their susceptibilities blunted by the exhibitions of boxers, fencers, or wild beasts; and the
Athenian manager would have been fined by the Court
of Areopagus, if he had not indeed been previously
stoned by the people, who should have affronted their

taste with the spectacle of Earthmen, African children,
or professors of the art of walking on the ceiling. Into
two little months was condensed every species of dramatic entertainment, from that of "gorgeous Tragedy,"
rivalling in its pomp and earnestness the ceremonials
of St. Peter's in Easter-week, to the satiric afterpiece
resembling in its extravagance the modern pantomime.
Tightly was the vessel hooped in, and effervescent accordingly were its contents. Neither must we measure an Athenian theatre in the season by any modern
comparisons. San Carlo, La Scala, and Her Majesty's
Theatre in the Haymarket, must hide their diminished
heads beside the theatre of the Athenian Iacchus.
Four thousand spectators would have " no room for
standing, miscalled standing-room," in the most capa-
cious European playhouse. Twenty thousand spectators were easily accommodated in the huge oval of the
Temple of Dionysus. And how discordant were the
ingredients of this enormous mass ! There was little
respect for persons in these assemblages. Cleon would
find himself seated beside his enemy the sausage-sel-
ler ; an elbow of stone divided Socrates from Anytus ;
and the noisest brawler of the Pnyx might be comfortably niched beside the decorous and the respectable
Nicias. The Government and the Opposition occupied
indiscriminate benches. There was the party clamorous for war, because it supplied the arsenal at the
Piræus with hemp, timber, and salt pork, mixed up
with the party clamorous for peace, because it could

no longer vend its figs and honey in the markets of
Thebes and Megara. The High-Temple party, which
denounced the philosophers as atheists, was placed
cheek-by-jowl with the free-thinking party, which
derided the priests as impostors; and there were the
young men, who cried up Euripides as the father of
wisdom, close packed with the old men, who abomi-
nated him as the father of lies.

For every class of the spectators, and to nearly
every individual among them, the Old Comedy yielded
entertainment and excitement. The demagogues applauded the caricature of Nicias and Demosthenes;
the aristocrats hailed with equal applause the portraiture of Cleon in 'The Knights.' The Sophists were
"shown up" in Socrates, pale, unshaven, meagre, and
meditative; the mathematicians in Meton; the soldiers,
full of strange oaths, and crested like game-cocks, in
Lamachus. And, like the modern Parisians, the
Athenians laughed heartily at themselves, as represented in the old dotard Demus, the victim of every
adviser who would take the trouble to pick his pockets.

But for such dramatic saturnalia, not freedom only,
but a high degree of external prosperity, was indispensable. So long as it waxed fat, the Athenian Demus
kicked lustily; so soon however as serious reverses
befell it, there came a long farewell to the license of
the stage, and to the zest for the Old Comedy. After
the disaster at Syracuse, the people began to look grave;
after its prostration at Ægospotami, jesting was not

to be thought of. The tyranny of the Thirty was indeed short-lived; yet although Thrasybulus restored their freedom, he could not give back to his countrymen their former cheer and alacrity. They had become a sadder, if not a wiser people; and indeed thenceforward there was little cause for extraordinary mirth. The assembly of the people shouted as of yore, when Demosthenes evoked the memory of the men of Marathon; but the contemporaries of Demosthenes no more resembled the heroes of Marathon and Salamis, than John Bright resembles Sir Philip Sidney. Athens had wrestled with and been thrown by Sparta, backed by the gold of the "great king." But a more formidable foe than either Sparta or Artaxerxes was now undermining Athens with his gold, and gathering round its borders with "war in procinct." A man of Macedon, whom Pericles would have deemed unworthy of a vote in the Agora, was now busy in the councils of the Athenians. Abroad they were ill served by impotent generals; at home they were betrayed by unjust stewards. The people had ceased to feel any strong or perdurable interest in the honour and dignity of the commonwealth. It hired soldiers to fight its battles, and mariners to row its galleys. Indolence whispered peace; and peace seemed to bring with it its own warrant, in the shape of exemption from invasion, of a steadier influx of money, of an increasing population, and greater leisure for amusement. The promptings of indolence were confirmed by the precepts of philosophy. The science of Theophrastus and the doctrines of Epicurus contributed equally to transform the jealous, irascible, and ambitious Athenians into a placid and studious people. The only eager contests henceforward raged in the philosophic schools: and it was thought more worthy of intelligent beings to define the *summum bonum*, or to reconcile the cravings of sense with the principles of duty, than to fix their yoke on Sicily and Carthage, or hold the balance between Thebes and Lacedæmon.

In every nation, one stage of society brings men of impassioned minds to the contemplation of manners, and of the social affections of man as exhibited in manners. With this propensity there doubtless co-operates some degree of despondency, whether as regards the political or the intellectual present. For politically, a nation must despond when it has become conscious to itself that its sinews of action are relaxed; and intellectually it cannot fail to droop when it has arrived at the conviction that the nerves and compass of its powers are shrunk and contracted. At this stage Athens had arrived in the fourth century before the Christian era; and under such circumstances arose the altered form of its dramatic literature.

We shall not pause upon the period of transition, the Middle Comedy. Like its predecessor, it dealt largely with personal satire; but the objects of satire were for the most part different. The laws and the altered, feelings of the Athenians alike forbade the dramatic poet to ridicule the pillars of the State. He accordingly fell foul of the philosophers who perplexed the young men with their paradoxes; or of the courtesans who ruined them by their extravagance. Plato stood in the place of Pericles; and Phrynè and Theano in those of Cleon and Nicias.

The audience at a representation of Menander's comedies differed in nearly every respect from that which had applauded Aristophanes and his rivals. In the course of half a century the political life of Athens had become nearly extinct; at least political sentiments were banished irrevocably from the stage. It was safe, so long as the Demus was in good spirits, and kept the purse of all the islands, to hold up to ridicule the great party-leaders; but it was ill jesting at the expense of a Macedonian Prefect, or at statesmen whom the Prefect would at any moment accommodate with a company of the Guard. The freedom of the theatre and of the assembly of the people had indeed expired together: and if Demosthenes had been forced by Antipater's agent to drink poison, a cup of hemlock was the least a poet could expect, who should presume to handle Antipater as Eupolis had treated Pericles. Moreover, the spectators who laughed at the license of the Old Comedy were almost exclusively Athenian, or such subjects of Athens as had made the city their permanent or casual abode. Most of them had dwelt long enough in Attica to imbibe all their virulence, both local and personal prejudices, and attended the theatre as partisans. The number also of the citizens was carefully limited; the meanest and poorest freeman plumed himself on his pure Ionian blood, and was chary of extending the franchise to aliens. His comedy was as national as himself; and, like himself, dealt in gross personalities. But after the Macedonians were established in Greece, the barriers of the Athenian franchise were thrown down. The people, ceasing to respect themselves, became prodigal of their privileges; and every adventurer who could bully or bribe them was certain of a statue and the freedom of the city for himself and his followers. Even kings had grown respectable in the estimation of the Athenians. The day had been when Dionysius of Syracuse had much ado to gain admission to the Olympian games. That point however was conceded in consideration of the splendid carriage-and-four he sent thither: the appearance and condition of his cattle subdued the tamers of horses. When however the same Dionysius sent a tragedy royal for representation at the Athenian festivals, the critics were inexorable, and the play was withdrawn under a perfect tempest of hisses and cat-calls. But in the second or third generation after, the citizens of Athens, or rather the mixed multitude that represented them, had become more polite. They allowed kings to court them: they came at last spontaneously to court kings. Presents of corn and wine from the Syrian Antiochi were

thankfully accepted; the gold and the compliments
of the Egyptian Ptolemies were exceedingly welcome:
there was a time, they thought, for all things; a time
to refuse, and a time to receive favours; a time to
tread on the neck of kings, and a time to erect statues
to them in the Pnyx. And in the age of Menander
the latter of these seasons had arrived.

The revolutions in the public life of Athens affected
the character of its literary men. A century before
the birth of Menander its historians had been statesmen, its philosophers legislators, and its poets generals or magistrates. With the Sophists began the
separation of the lives practical and contemplative.
As regarded Athens, the Sophists were mostly aliens
by birth, who could exercise no function of the State;
and their gains as lecturers *de omni scibili* were increased by their independence of secular business, and
by their privilege of locomotion. Socrates, the most
practical of teachers, took his share bravely in all civil
and military duties; but on his disciple Plato the
mantle of the Sophists, in one respect, descended.
For the chief of the Academy was the first who
broached the questionable doctrine that it was the
duty of the philosopher to abstain from political employments; and the precepts of the master were carried
out by his scholar Aristotle, both in spirit and in
letter. The poets were not behindhand in claiming
the privilege of seclusion. Euripides, who, as we shall
see presently, approached the New Comedy in propor-

tion as he receded from the Elder Drama, was an author by profession; and in the age of Demosthenes, as we learn from the reiterated complaints of the orator himself, there was an increasing scarcity of men willing to devote their wealth and talents to the service of the State. When Menander began to write, the separation of the literary from the political world of Athens was nearly complete.

In Menander's generation, accordingly, we encounter a new phase of Athenian society,—a phase familiar enough in our own days, but unknown, or at least so unusual as to have escaped record, in the high and palmy days of the democracy. We then meet for the first time with the well-born and wealthy Athenian gentleman, whose public duties were fulfilled by the regular payment of his rates and taxes, by an occasional "turn-out" with the city militia, and an occasional attendance as juryman. Coarser or more ambitious spirits might wrangle in the public assembly, or covet diplomatic errands to Pella and Rhodes, or impair their patrimonies by equipping a troop of horse or a trireme. The utmost that a gentleman could be expected to do for his country's service was now and then to present one of its philosophical institutions with a talent or so, or to subscribe handsomely to a tragic chorus. Nor did his seclusion from public offices expose him to the charge of lukewarm patriotism. That virtue indeed had pretty nearly expired with Demosthenes; and there was little in the ex-

ternal or internal condition of Athens after the battle
of Chæroncia to prompt or sustain self-sacrifice for the
commonwealth. The Athenians sought a master, and
found many masters: like estates with damaged titles,
they rapidly changed owners; Demetrius the Phale-
rian was their idol one day, and Demetrius the "Town-
taker" their idol the next; until their mutability was
fixed and congealed for ever by the preponderance
first of Macedon, and afterwards of Rome.

The career of Menander, so far as it is known, illustrates the political decay of Athens. His father, Dio-
peithes, had done the State some service as a General; and had been honoured equally by the friendship
of Demosthenes and the enmity of the Macedonian
party. The son however trod not in his father's
footsteps. His paternal uncle was a dramatic writer
of no mean repute, and from him Menander probably
imbibed his predilections for the stage. His means
were ample; his education was carefully superintended
by his relative; and from Theophrastus, the favourite
pupil of Aristotle, he learned not only to prefer the
service of the Muses to that of the State, but also
to mark the qualities of mankind with a learned eye.
The "*Characters*" of Theophrastus, the original parent
and model of Earle, La Bruyère, and so many prose
satirists, were admirable lessons for one destined to
hold up the mirror of life to his contemporaries; while
the encyclopædic studies of his tutor were well adapted
to cherish the faculties of observation and compa-

rison. The poet was equally felicitous in the choice of his friend. The elder tragic drama had dealt with the sublime truths or hypotheses of religion, with the struggles between fate and free-will, with the opposition between man and destiny, or with the strife between the Gods of Olympus—the established creed of Greece—and the earlier worship of the elements. The Elder Comedy had disported itself equally with the superstitions of the multitude and the theories of the philosophers. It laughed at Jupiter; it laughed at Socrates; and it inculcated generally that it was better to eat, drink, and be merry, than to burn incense or to sacrifice calves, or go pale and unshaven in quest of speculative truth. The New Comedy, while it reserved to itself the indispensable privilege of ridiculing all and sundry, whether their abode were on Olympus, or in the Academy, required a system of morals differing alike from that of Æschylus and that of Aristophanes. Fate and free-will were too grave for it; mirth and physical enjoyment too coarse and indiscriminate. Dealing principally with the domestic life of man, it demanded also an ethical system which rested mainly on the domestic affections. The philosophy of Epicurus, apart from its physical speculations, afforded such a system; and Epicurus was the bosom-friend of Menander. The poet had entered his second year when the philosopher was born; their friendship was uninterrupted; their studies converged towards a common centre, since the object of each was man : and Menander, with real or affected enthusiasm, compares his friend to Themistocles ; since the one had giv n *freedom*, and the other *wisdom*, to Athens. The writings of Aristotle confirmed the oral instructions of Theophrastus and Epicurus. The critical and ethical doctrines of the Stageirite were embodied in the co-medies of Menander, and we can trace in his verses the influence of his tutors; for while he insinuates or enforces the milder sentiments of the Garden, he indulges in occasional sallies against the doubts of the Academy and the eccentricities of the Porch.

Menander however did not derive his knowledge of human character from philosophic sages alone; he studied it in the more attractive form of refined female society. We do not mean to imply by this phrase that Menander was either in the main a person of strict life and conversation, or blest with a good wife. Of such conversation we believe there was little enough in Athens at the time; and a good wife was hardly to be had for love or money. The condition of women in Greece nearly forbade the existence of such a prodigy. The wife was the mistress of her servants, and the head nurse of her children; but she was not, and she could not be, the companion and friend of her husband. Born, educated, and kept through life in a state of almost oriental seclusion, the Greek wife was necessarily illiterate, unintellectual, and, except for her beauty or her dower, unattractive. To dress, to gossip, and to eat confectionery, were her highest

pleasures; she would have subjected herself to divorce,
had she appeared at the theatre, the games, or the
philosophical schools; and her partner would have
deemed it an inexpiable portent, if his better half had
cited a verse of Sophocles, or questioned him con-
cerning an opinion of Zeno's. The blue-stockings of
Athens were for the most part of servile origin, but
selected in childhood for the promise of their beauty
or their gifts; and, according to the prejudices of the
age, *unsexed*, before they became the equal compa-
nions of man. Hence arose a capital defect in the
Athenian drama. In the *répertoire* of female characters, the women are either furies, vixens, or statuesque
abstractions. Of all Shakespeare's women, Lady Macbeth, Goneril, and Regan, would alone have been intelligible to a Greek spectator. Juliet, Imogen, and
Hermione would have been enigmas to him. He
would have approved Petruchio's discipline, and Iago's
insinuations. Beatrice and Rosalind he would assuredly have put down for hetæræ—no better than
they should be.

While Menander was writing verses under his
uncle's tuition, or noting with Theophrastus the fops,
bullies, and misers of his native city, a lady of this
order was causing no slight sensation among the fashionable circles of Antioch. She was the all-potent
mistress of Harpalus, the Macedonian Prefect of Syria.
He had raised to her a statue of bronze in the laurel
groves of Daphne by Orontes; at Tarsus he allotted

to her apartments in the palace of the Pasargadæ; for her sake he had relieved her native Athens during a season of dearth by a liberal donation of corn; and he had publicly announced that he would refuse every votive crown from the provincials, unless a similar offering adorned the fair brow of his companion. The antechamber of the beautiful Athenian was crowded with suitors; heads were bowed and knees were bent as her chariot passed through the streets; and so long as Harpalus retained the favour of Alexander, Glycera was hailed as a queen throughout Syria and the Lesser Asia.

To descend from a Prefect's palace to a poet's lodging may argue some decline of fortune; yet if we may credit the scandalous chronicles of the day, Glycera was not ill-lodged under Menander's roof. Assuredly, though he produced at least one hundred and five comedies, he did not live by his wits; for he is recorded to have fared sumptuously every day, and to have been prodigal in his dress and fond of exquisite perfumes. Long after Menander and his mistress had done with the cares or luxuries of life, a writer of imaginary letters composed in their names certain epistles which we agree with M. Guizot in thinking entitled to some degree of credit, so far at least as regards the traditions embodied in them. Alciphron, the author of the letters, possessed ample means of learning the literary gossip of Athens; and so celebrated a poet as Menander, who was besides a man

of fashion and a wit, certainly left behind him some
rumours of his manners as well as of his genius.
And we are the more inclined to allow to these letters
a semi-historical credit, in consideration of the genuine tenderness and delicacy exhibited in them. A
mere forgery is generally very clumsy work. The
Epistles of Phalaris, for example, and most of those
ascribed to Plato, betray their spuriousness by their
stupidity. But through the language of Alciphron
appear gleams of natural feeling, that argue something beyond the invention of an entire stranger to
the correspondents. And even historically they are
valuable, inasmuch as they presuppose circumstances
illustrative of the literary condition of Greece in that
age. It was no new thing for a Greek historian or
poet to be a banished man. Æschylus was the victim
of ostracism, and found refuge at the court of Hiero;
Euripides paid the penalty of his philosophic speculations by exile under the roof of the Macedonian
king, Archelaus; and Thucydides wrote his account
of the defeat of Athens at Syracuse, under a plane-
tree on the coast of Thrace. But these were enforced
absences from the neighbourhood of all that was dear
in the world to an Athenian, and the bread was bitter
which they ate, even though a king gave it ungrudg-
ingly. Although however the guests of monarchs, they
were not invited guests. Nor until the Macedonian
conquests had extended Greece over Asia, and erected
libraries and academies in barbaric Syria and Egypt,

do we meet with any traces of royal patronage to the
learned.   In Menander's age Athens was no longer
the University of the civilized world.   Egypt strove
with Syria in inviting, and, what was still more to the
purpose, in pensioning, poets and historians; and the
Ptolemies especially had drawn around them a galaxy
of wits. Ptolemy Philopator with his own royal hand
indited letters to Philemon and Menander; and the
latter exultingly tells Glycera that the invitation to
Philemon was the less pressing of the two. The King
was indeed liberal, since he promised Menander " all
the wealth in the world."   But the poet gallantly
assures his mistress that for all the gold under the
moon he will not quit Athens, since Athens alone
contains Glycera. She might indeed accompany him;
the court of Egypt was in no respect prudish or particular : but he will not expose her to perils by water,
nor to the discomfort of dwelling in a strange land.
Glycera replies with equal warmth and *abandon ;* but
as we have not room for more of these effusions, we
heartily recommend our readers to peruse them, either
in the choice Greek of Alciphron, or in M. Guizot's
version.   They are by many degrees more entertain-
ing than the Grenville Correspondence, and have in
them a certain flavour of *Eloise* that renders them
none the worse.

The invitation of Ptolemy is authentic, even if the
constancy of Menander to Glycera be apocryphal;
and it points to a revolution in the literary condition

of Greece. It indicates indeed the *third* phase of
Hellenic literature. At first, like the race which produced it, that literature was broken up into distinct
nationalities. The Ionians appropriated to themselves
epic poetry; the Bœotians, an uninventive practical
people, applauded the sound didactic good-sense of
Hesiod, who gave them excellent advice when to sow
and when to reap, when to expect fair weather and
when to look out for rain, or catalogued their Gods as
methodically as if he had meant to put Zeus, Herè,
and Kronos up to auction. The Æolians and Dorians reflected their national characteristics in lyrical
composition, yet with a difference, the susceptible Æolians running over every chord of passion, the earnest
and warlike Dorians touching only the sublimer strings
of religious emotion. Paros gave birth to the sharp-
edged Iambic verse, hereafter appropriated to dramatic dialogue, but at first confined to satirical invective. The Dorians of Megara and Sicily, softened
and enlivened probably by their commercial intercourse with strangers, relaxed their "Dorian mood"
and invented comedy. Tragedy, by an equal anomaly,
originated with the cheerful and volatile Athenians;
while Miletus enjoyed for many years a monopoly of
historians and philosophers.

The era of nationalities in literature was broken up
by the results of the Persian War. Athens sprang
up so vigorously from her prostration by Xerxes, that
henceforward she became for a century and a half the

intellectual centre of Greece. Paris in the eighteenth
century was not more entirely the *arbiter eleganti-
arum* for Europe, than Athens during this era was
for Greece. No other dialect than pure Attic was
endurable in civilized speech or writing. The broad
tones of the Dorians were derided by the critical
world, as the broad Scotch of King James's courtiers was derided by the English Euphuists. The
Bœotians bleated; the Arcadians brayed; the Ionians
whistled; the Macedonians spoke like the barbarous
Triballians; and the language of every Asiatic people
was compared to the shriek of bats or the bellowing
of kine. The literature of Athens was no less exclu-
sive than its language. If the fables of its dramas
were borrowed from the legends of Thebes or Mycenæ,
the *dénouement* of the plot usually centred in Athens
itself. Œdipus must die, and Orestes be cleansed
from blood in the grove of the Attic Eumenides, or at
the tribunal of the Attic Areopagus. Thither is Medea
borne in her dragon-car; there Danaus and his daugh-
ters at length find rest, after "their weary wanderings
long." The central figure in the historical groups of
the Dorian Herodotus is the city of Pallas; and the
security or redemption of her greatness is the theme
of all the orators. Sparta, Thebes, and Argos have
no historians. Are not their wars and their revolutions written in the books of the Athenians alone?

But the monopoly of Athens, intellectually as well
as politically, ceased so soon as Greece once again

poured itself forth upon Asia, and re-acted the destruction of Troy in the conquest of Babylon and the East. The Attic dialect was thenceforward the dialect of learned purists alone. The Ionian and Dorian speech was revived and modified by Callimachus, Apollonius, and Theocritus; and the Fellows of the Alexandrian University prided themselves upon their familiarity with the archaisms of Homer and Pindar. For all ordinary purposes, men were content to write in the language which they spoke; and although, for their convenient and subtle mechanism, they adhered to Attic forms in dramatic composition, even the learned no longer recoiled from Hellenistic phrases, as from the *patois* of the workshop and the market-place.

One or two anecdotes of Menander's life remain to be noticed before we proceed to the consideration of his writings. We are afraid that either his or Glycera's constancy did not last to the end of their lives. Mention is made of a lady named Bacchis; and of her, if Alciphron did not maliciously invent the slander, Glycera was decidedly jealous. She writes a very urgent note to Bacchis, conjuring her by their friendship not to be too gracious to her lover, who is perversely bent on accompanying Bacchis to the next Isthmian games. She adds—"He is so devilishly given to fall in love, that if you *can* manage to bring him back from Corinth tolerably affectionate to me, I shall always consider myself your deeply obliged." Whether Menander returned as desired, we do not know.

c

But a worse matter than the journey in Bacchis's company is intimated. There is an awkward fragment in which the poet speaks plainly of Bacchis as very dear to him. And then Philemon, Menander's rival in public favour, must needs take to commending Glycera on the stage as a good kind of woman! Whereupon her lover as publicly replied, " She is nothing of the sort." And so, after these almost unmistakable symptoms of a quarrel direct, Glycera and Bacchis vanish into utter darkness.

Once, though prudently abstaining from politics, Menander appears to have got into a decided scrape with great men. He had been in high favour with Demetrius of Phalerum; but unluckily that Demetrius had his day, and his namesake, who bore the terrible appellation of " Town-taker," became lord and master of Athens. The " Town-taker" knew not and cared nothing for Menander. Here was an opportunity for taking the conceit out of a popular author. And it was not lost. For incontinently an information was laid against Menander as a member of the Opposition; and it would doubtless have fared ill with him, since the " Town-taker" was by no means scrupulous about fines, imprisonment, or even a dose of hemlock, when a certain cousin of Demetrius the Second interceded for him, and the information was quashed.

He was not, however, destined to die in the course of nature, or to complete his 106th comedy; for in the fifty-second year of his age, he was drowned in the harbour of Piræus. There was no Poet's Corner in Athens; but his countrymen erected to him a tomb on the road from the sea to the town, and it was seen in the second century of our era by Pausanias, who, like Weever, delighted in noting down the "Funeral Monuments" of Grecian worthies.

"To be read by bare inscriptions like many in Gruter, to be studied by antiquaries who we were, are cold consolations unto the students of perpetuity," says Sir Thomas Browne. Menander's fame, so far as regards his writings, rests upon little more than a few disjointed fragments preserved by the grammarians as examples of Attic diction, or cited incidentally by heathen moralists and Christian divines. Yet his reputation is as authentic as if we held in our hands a succession of his scenes, or even some of his entire plays.

Superstition has ever been a greater foe to letters than barbarism. We owe the loss of Menander's plays to the stupidity of the Byzantine priests. Until the very end of the twelfth century it was possible to procure nearly a complete copy of them; but after that period they disappear. A holocaust of precious manuscripts was offered to the fanaticism of the Emperors; and Menander and the new comedy, Alcæus and lyrical poetry, were destroyed, in order that the tedious verses of Gregory of Nazianzum might be alone read in the schools. The vitality of Menander's

name is owing chiefly to his having been the model of
Terence, who translated, combined, and modified his
dramas for the Roman theatre. The Terentian Menander, which, with all its elegances, bears about the
same relation to the Greek original that Schlegel's
version of Shakespeare bears to the English text,
after delighting the aristocratical circles of Rome,
passed with Roman literature into the library of modern Europe. There it became the parent of an
innumerable progeny, and reckons among its descendants Molière's 'Tartuffe' and Sheridan's 'School for
Scandal.'

The New Comedy of Greece, indeed, was much
better suited than its elder drama to planting offsets
in theatrical literature. It was, as we have already
seen, much less national in its texture, both as regarded the manners which it portrayed and the ideas
which it developed. The habits and opinions of refined society are nearly alike in every nation at similar
periods of civilization : the number of characters is
limited, since conventionality produces few varieties.
The *répertoire* of the Menandrian comedy is restricted
to the following generic forms :—the severe and the
indulgent father; the cunning and the stolid slave; the
son who is his father's favourite and a scapegrace; and
a less-favoured son, who is a respectable character;
the extravagant courtesan; the shrewish wife; the
bragging soldier; the parasite, whose business is to
flatter for his dinner; the freed-woman, who is gene-

rally a nurse or a procuress; and the free or slave girl, who is the subject of the love intrigue, but who, from the difficulty of representing female characters on the Greek stage, is often a mute person, and sometimes does not appear on the scene at all. As the Greeks lived so much in public, nearly all the theatrical business is transacted in the street or the market-place; for it would have been inconsistent with the manners of Menander's age, to represent scenes within the house at a period when there was hardly any domestic life, except at the lodgings of the Hetæræ.

A history of Greek manners might indeed be almost compiled from the fragments of the New Comedy, aided by the unmutilated dramas of Plautus and Terence. In the first place, the Bobadils of the Greek stage represent a class of soldiers which, in the piping times of peace, overran and infested every Hellenic city. As national feeling died out in the republics, the employment of mercenary soldiers became a general practice; who, when not enlisted by any leader of *condottieri*, sauntered about—the fashionable guardsmen of the day. To parents and guardians these captains and colonels were of course objects of dread and aversion: they were the victims of the Hetæræ so long as they had money in their purse; and they were the prey of all who lived by their wits, of the parasite who flattered for a dinner, and of the cunning slave who delighted in the *rôle* of the unjust steward. The later wars of Athens had not only brought with

them sweeping social changes, but also had materially
affected its commerce.   Hence, though individuals
were richer, and less exposed to the arts of informers
than formerly, the mass of the Athenian people were
poorer, since they could no longer find employment in
the wharfs of Munychium or the dockyards of Piræus.
The public *largesse*—the profits of her dominion over
the islands—was also greatly curtailed, and where
men can find no honest employment, nor be supported
as state-paupers, the dull must starve, while the clever
will live by their wits.   The buffoon of Aristophanes
became the parasite of Menander; and each represents
in his respective age a different epoch of manners.
The free Athenian was gluttonous, sensual, and ob-
trusive: the degenerated Athenian retained the sensuality of his forefathers; but bowed, lied, and flattered
in order to indulge in it.

A common *dénoûment* in the New Comedy is the
discovery that the slave-girl, whose intrigue with the
heir of the family forms the staple of the plot, is really
the daughter of a respectable household, who had been
carried off by corsairs in her infancy, and then sold
in the slave-market.   The Greeks were in all ages ad-
dicted to robbing on the high seas.   Even now the
Archipelago swarms with petty pirates, who plunder
the farms and vineyards of the islands, lie in wait for
the market-boats, and carry off Greek children to the
harems of the Asiatic Turks.   The naval supremacy
of Athens for more than a century kept these water-

rats in tolerable order; but so soon as that supremacy declined, the Ægean again swarmed with marauders. Hence no casualty was more common in Menander's age than the loss of a child, or even of an entire nursery. And the recurrence of such discoveries of offspring on the stage, though it is one of the pleasant absurdities of Sheridan's 'Critic,' appeared a matter of course to the spectators of Menander. Lastly, in proportion as Athens ceased to be a maritime and commercial power, the agricultural habits of the population returned; and hence we meet in the New Comedy with so many allusions to the farms abounding with pigs, honey, and millet, and find so many traces of a bucolical turn of mind in fathers of families.

The Athenians were in all ages a sententious race, loving curt ethical maxims, proverbs, and epigrammatic conceits. The plays of Euripides, who in some respects was the model of the later comic writers, abound in aphorisms, and are often tedious from their dialectic point and formality. Perhaps no peculiarity has more tended to the preservation of the fragments of the New Comedy than the frequency of gnomic sentences. Its aphorismal wisdom or sagacity recommended it equally to the practical Romans and to the saints and fathers of the Church. Here at least the new religion might borrow from the old, since good sense or good morals benefit all mankind. In the absence of any entire drama of this period, it

is rash to speculate upon the leading characteristics of
its authors; but to judge from the fragments, we are
inclined to think that shrewd observations on the
motives and principles of men in daily life were quite
as remarkable as skill in dramatic plot, or as the
powers of fancy or imagination. Menander, in spite
of his luxurious mode of living, appears to have been
a man of conspicuously sound sense, and to have
studied all human qualities with a most learned eye.
His opportunities for observation were of the first
order. His days were passed in the highest circles
of a city whither flocked, even in its decline, persons
from nearly every quarter of the civilized world, in
pursuit of gain, instruction, or pleasure. The philosophical schools alone yearly attracted hundreds of
students to the lecture-rooms of the four greater sects.
Hither resorted also the amateurs of art, and the
professional sculptor and painter. In a dialogue of
Lucian's, written nearly three hundred years after
the latest of Menander's comedies, we meet with a
Roman gentleman congratulating himself upon having in his youth quitted the noise, the smoke, and the
tumult of the metropolis of Italy for the seclusion of
Athens. From the same writer, who is among the
best historians of social life, we learn that the Piræus
was second only to Alexandria as a common centre
for the various races of mankind. To that port came
the Syrian silk-merchants of Antioch; the corn-factors
of Egypt; the Parthian with his cargo of Indian spices;

the negro in the train of the Roman prætor or proconsul; the Iberian with his consignment of silver and iron; and the Massilian Gaul with the wines of Narbonne. In Menander's days, the crowd was less diversified, but hardly less numerous; and there are vestiges in his fragments of a liberal employment of these human groups in his comedies.

We had intended to lay before our readers an outline at least of one of Menander's comedies; but our space is exhausted, and we must content ourselves with referring them to the treatise of M. Guillaume Guizot. To our apprehension, the history of wars and treaties is often tedious and uninstructive, representing one phase only, and that among the most uniform, of the human species. Much more interesting and instructive is it to trace the identity of man under the thin disguises of manners and costume; to discern under the tunic and the toga the passions, follies, and virtues which still actuate Mayfair and Whitechapel; and to discover that the distinction between Christian and pagan life consists rather in the development of man's moral and intellectual nature, than in the superficial and accidental aspect of new creeds and new forms of society. If our readers agree with us on this point, we have rendered them some service in directing their attention for a few moments to the " Life and Times of Menander."

BEAUMONT AND FLETCHER.*

—◆—

WE are at length enabled to read Beaumont and
Fletcher with the aid of a well-restored or corrected
text, and of a full but not burdensome commentary.
The careless manner in which these playwrights, in
common with their dramatic brethren, were originally printed, has hitherto been very imperfectly
amended by successive editors. Of the three critical
editions of their plays which preceded Mr. Dyce's,
Weber's alone (1812) has any pretensions to merit
on the score of editorial competence. Of Seward and
Sympson (1750) it may be said that nearly all they
did without the help of Theobald's 'Adversaria' was
done amiss; and the chief value of the edition of
1778, generally known as Colman's edition, arises
from its having cancelled most of their interpolations and conjectures, and restored the capricious

* Reprinted from 'Fraser's Magazine,' March, 1850.
The Works of Beaumont and Fletcher. With Notes, and a Bio-
graphical Memoir. By the Rev. Alexander Dyce. 11 vols. 8vo.
London. Moxon, 1843–46.
The Works of Beaumont and Fletcher. With an Introduction.
By George Darley. 2 vols. 8vo. Moxon, 1840.

yet frequently preferable text of the folios and quartos. The tender mercies of their editors have, indeed, been often as fatal to the sense or the metre of these poets, as were his two wives to the middle-aged gentleman in Æsop. The one plucked out his white hairs and the other his black, until between them he was left bald.

The present age seems favourable to the revival of Beaumont and Fletcher's reputation. Several of their dramas have been recently brought again upon the stage, and two editions of their entire works have been put forth by that classical and enterprising publisher, Mr. Moxon. It did not fall within Mr. Darley's commission to revise the text of his authors, but his Introduction is a spirited and ingenious commentary on their lives and writings. The student of English poetry, who already owes so much to Mr. Dyce for his editions of Peele, Marlowe, Middleton, and Skelton, will gladly welcome his labours on Beaumont and Fletcher. To his skill in old books and archaic lore, Mr. Dyce brings the rarer adjuncts of sound judgment and good taste. He applies to our native literature the erudition and acumen which distinguished Porson among Greek scholars. We know not indeed where to look for a more appropriate parallel. Mr. Dyce is at once copious in his resources and cautious in his emendations. His ear for metre is fine; his detection of obscure or doubtful meanings is sagacious. He is frugal of comment, while he is familiar with whatever in print or manuscript elucidates his authors. He does not, like so many of the earlier school of Shakespeare-commentators, use the poets as a stalking-horse for his own learning and ingenuity. He is as laborious as Malone, without his dulness; and as acute as Steevens, without his malice. He does not wage in his notes private wars with his brother annotators, nor does he, like Warton, find parallels between Macedon and Monmouth, or like Gifford, affect a surly superciliousness towards all who may chance to differ from him. No specimens or extracts would convey to a reader not previously aware of the state of Beaumont and Fletcher's text, the amount of his obligations to their recent editor. From his appreciation of particular plays we may occasionally dissent; but we bear unhesitating testimony to the accuracy and diligence, the ability and good taste, with which Mr. Dyce has executed his present task.

Mr. Dyce's researches have thrown fresh light on the personal history of the poets and on the sources and bibliography of their plays. In the latter department he has remodelled and much improved upon former investigations, even where he has not added to them. There is still some obscurity attached to the origin of many of Fletcher's plots. We incline to think that a closer study of the Spanish novelists and playwrights would lead to further discoveries of their sources. Mr. Dyce, indeed, states his "conviction that our early playwrights very seldom made use of foreign *dramas*." There is, however, an earnestness and rhetorical amplitude in the Spanish comedy which must have been attractive to the brother poets, to the grave and *judicious* Beaumont especially; and there are resemblances in the plan and conduct of their dramas, in the first acts of their comedies especially, which point to the Spanish *stage* as well as the Spanish novelists. They can have been under no obligations to Calderon, yet both in tragedy and comedy they remind us of him and of his contemporary, Corneille. The hero of genteel comedy, and his friend or rival, the pairs of lovers and the pairs of valets, the prevalence of wit and banter over humour, the vigour of the first act in comparison with the succeeding acts, the loose texture and frequent incongruities of the plot, are Spanish features. The resemblance is even closer in those plays in which Greek or Roman characters are introduced; for example, in Calderon's 'La Gran Cenobia' and Fletcher's 'Prophetess.' The poetic element is stronger than the dramatic: the outline is weak, the ornaments are gorgeous. We should be glad to see this question examined by some scholar well versed in the writings of Lope di Vega and his contemporaries. It is almost the only unworked vein of illustration for the English drama.

Mr. Dyce's remarks upon the critical and dramatic character of the several plays are comprised in his 'Account of the Lives and Writings' of their authors;

and each play has besides a separate introduction containing its original story, where the source is known,
and its scenic and literary history. The practice of
tacking a moral summary to dramas is happily defunct. We could never stomach the entrance of Dr.
Johnson to comment upon Lear's madness or Benedick's marriage. It is much worse to read Dr. Ireland's sermons on Massinger. Not content with being
monitory out of his pulpit, the doctor apologizes for
sitting in judgment on a playwright at all. He is
much too good, he intimates, for such employments.
"Out upon such half-faced fellowship!" Mr. Dyce
has juster notions of an editor's duties. What his
hand found to do therein, he has done with all his
might, and he leaves the reader to extract his own
moral. The bias of Fletcher's mind to prurient sentiments and images, his fondness for the debatable
ground between virtue and vice, his microscopic trials
of a foible or an emotion, are palpable enough without an editor's proclaiming them. We would not
excuse these faults—blemishes alike in the man and
the artist, but there should be allowance in the verdict. Beaumont and Fletcher wrote for " worshipful
society." The hearing and the reading public of the
seventeenth century had in these poets and in their
contemporaries and successors *their* Balzacs and Eu-
gène Sues, *their* 'Jack Sheppards' and 'Mysteries' of
society—*Mutato nomine . . . fabula narratur:* our ancestors tolerated grossness; we endure and applaud sen-

timental and melodramatic fiction. It was not merely
the London 'prentices and sempstresses who crowded
round the cart and gallows of Mrs. Turner; it was
not only a rustic or city populace that thronged and
scrambled before the scaffold of Rush. "The king,
the queen, the courtiers," in Fletcher's age, applauded
the language of the scene as an echo of the language
of the palace. The State-trials in James's reign—a
small fraction of current offences—attest the moral
corruption and anomalous vices of the age. In that
corruption and in those vices Carr and Villiers par-
ticipated. They were denounced from the pulpit by
Donne and Andrews, they were proven at the bar
before Coke and Bacon. The stage may have added
to the impurities of the stream: it did not originally
corrupt the fountain.

So much has been written of late upon Beaumont
and Fletcher, that in examining their scenic and poetic
character, however briefly, we can hardly avoid pre-
occupied ground. But their literary dimensions are
ample enough to admit of recurrence, and the station
they have so long held among playwrights warrants
successive attempts to analyze their merits. Mr. Hallam remarks that Fletcher's verses are seldom cited,
and have no enduring hold on the memory. Would
not his observation apply to all our elder dramatists
except Shakespeare? and even in his case quotations
are rare from 'Timon' and 'Pericles,' the 'Comedy of
Errors,' or 'All's Well that Ends Well.' We are living

in a period of much literary oblivion as well as of much
literary production. The Bickerstaff family, with all
their pleasant eccentricities, have given place to Elia,
'Robinson Crusoe' has a formidable rival in 'Mas-
terman Ready,' and to most readers under thirty
Sir Roger de Coverley himself is almost as much a
stranger as the heroes and heroines of 'Parthenia' and
the 'Grand Cyrus.' That so few of Beaumont and
Fletcher's fifty-two dramas are remembered, is therefore, in Philosopher Square's phrase, rather "in the
eternal nature of things," than a proof of their inferiority. The very bulk of their works is adverse to
familiarity with their contents. If we take away the
four plays which Porson rendered necessary to the
scholar, Euripides, the best preserved and the most
voluminous, is the least known of the classical play-
writers. But that Beaumont and his colleague, amid
all the caprices of fashion and under successive tides
of literature, should have remained "steadfast starres"
in the dramatic firmament is a token of sterling worth,
however incommensurate their present reputation may
be with their contemporary popularity.

Whether it were from this cause or from the tena-
city of a few of their plays on the stage, their names
have always held the next rank to Shakespeare and
Jonson, while Chapman, Marston, Dekker, and Webster, poets of deeper though less varied powers, have
been rescued from oblivion almost within the present
century, and chiefly through the criticisms of Charles

Lamb. Lamb's pregnant and suggestive notes led not indirectly to the editorial labours of Gifford and Mr. Dyce. Beaumont and Fletcher have, indeed, suffered occasional eclipse. Goldsmith, in a pleasant vein of irony, observes that his age had turned aside from Dryden and Otway, and "gone back a whole century" to Fletcher and Shakespeare. Such coupling of names by the most genial critic of the Johnsonian era is no ordinary tribute to the younger of these poets. We know from Pepys that, immediately after the Restoration, Beaumont and his colleague were highly popular. The first play, indeed, acted on the re-opening of the theatres in 1650—'The Humourous Lieutenant'—was a production of Fletcher's. Dryden asserts that for one of Shakespeare's, two of their plays used to be acted in his time; and manager Cibber confirms Dryden's and Pepys' statement, although the prose comedy of Wycherley, Vanbrugh, and Congreve was rapidly displacing their poetic predecessors. We believe the period of their greatest obscuration extends from about the accession of James II. to the close of Queen Anne's reign. From the latter of these dates we find frequent attempts to reproduce their dramas on the stage. Monmouth's rebellion and William's disputed title to the crown may have furnished political reasons for withdrawing pieces in which usurpers and pretenders to thrones are so frequently introduced. The fashion of after-pieces may also have been unfavourable to dramas of such length, and making such demands on the actors, as those of Beaumont and Fletcher. In the interim, they were out-ranted by Lee, surpassed in extravagance and indecency by Dryden, repelled by frigid Catos and Jane Shores, plundered without detection by manufacturers of plays, and adapted without acknowledgment by managers of theatres. For "these effects defective" causes may be found in the varying taste or prejudices of successive generations.

"The written life of a great poet," says Mr. Darley, "is often far duller than the written life of a great blockhead. The latter, through mere mental unfitness for meditative pursuits, plunges blind amidst life's many vortices, to attain the pleasure, the profit, or the excitement from without he cannot have from within; while the poet's deeds are his *works* — his explorements and excursions into the world of reflection and imagination."

Certainly many of Fletcher's contemporaries, blockheads or not, whether they went in quest of El Dorado with Raleigh, or fought under the Lion of the North like Sir Dugald Dalgetty, or noted down with Sir Symonds D'Ewes the routine business of the Commons, could have told more of the world and its ways than either Beaumont or his colleague. Yet the biographies of the latter are not therefore void of instruction and interest. Their friendship is touching, their fortunes were not unlike, their intellectual structures were congenial. In an age when dramatic co-part-

nerships were common, their poetic union was noted
for its permanence and intimacy. "In the most high
and palmy state" of our elder drama, says Mr. Dyce,
"when the demand for novelty was almost incessant,
it is well known that more than one playwright was
frequently employed by a manager to labour on the
same piece." Fletcher was so associated with Rowley
and Middleton, with Massinger and Shirley, and possibly with Shakespeare himself. "But there seems to
be no doubt that the literary partnership which has
given immortality to the united names of Beaumont
and Fletcher was altogether different — that it was
formed and continued at their own free choice, and
not at the pleasure of a theatrical proprietor." "There
was," Aubrey tells us, "a wonderful consimility of
phansy" between them. The *idem velle et nolle* extended to their dress, lodging, and diet, and in one
particular, for which we must refer the reader to Mr.
Dyce for the fact and to Ariosto for a parallel, it tran-
scended all Cicero's rules of True Friendship. The
"consimility of phansy" may have been fostered by si-
milarity of circumstances. Both were sons of men of
worship. Beaumont's father was a judge; Fletcher's
was a bishop. The education of both was completed
in "seminaries of sound learning;" Fletcher's at
Bene't College, and Beaumont's at Broadgate Hall,
now Pembroke College, Cambridge. Both, too, came
of a poetical stock. There were three Fletcher poets
beside the dramatist, and five Beaumonts. Of the

Fletchers, Giles and Phineas are still remembered as
the authors respectively, of 'Christ's Victory and
Triumph'—a poem which Milton laid under contribution; and of the 'Purple Island'—a poem at once
anatomical and allegorical.   Of the Beaumonts, Sir
John, the father of Francis the dramatist, was the
author of 'Bosworth Field' and other poems, which
have been commended by Mr. Wordsworth for their
"spirit, elegance, and harmony;" and a kinsman, Dr.
Joseph Beaumont, wrote 'Psyche, or Love's Mystery'
—a work from which Pope counselled young authors
to steal.   Nor was the intellectual vein worn out in
that generation.   The present century has produced
few more accomplished gentlemen, and none worthier
of a poetic genealogy, than the late Sir George Beaumont, of the Colorton branch of the family; and
Francis Beaumont's mother, a Pierrepoint, connects
the family with Lady Mary Wortley Montague.   Cowper in like manner came of a tuneful race.   There are
two stout octavos of occasional verses, for the most
part by his near kindred, which will bear comparison
with any "pieces by Persons of Quality."   Hand-
writing, musical talents, and "the accomplishment of
verse," frequently run in families; and should at
length a genuine poet spring from the stock, while
he illustrates, he is indebted to it for the transmis-
sion of the "vein."   Sensibility to metrical harmony
implies a finer organization than common; and if the
poet inherit nothing more from his race than a pre-

disposition to sweet sounds, he owes to it one of the prime elements of his maturer genius. Nor should the ermine of the judge and the lawn of the bishop be omitted in recounting the formative accidents of the career of these poets. There is a stateliness even in their lighter moods of comedy, a conventionality in their banter, which bespeak reminiscences at least of the state and ceremonies of juridical and episcopal housekeeping. They were alike in other matters. Both were handsome men. Mr. Darley says that English poets have generally been so. He is perhaps not altogether an unbiassed witness, since he has written some excellent verses himself; but he forgets Jonson, Goldsmith, and Churchill. Both too were famous for their conversational powers, "being," as a contemporary wrote, "so fluent as to talk a comedy," and therefore among the very choicest spirits at the Mermaid in Friday Street.

Such were some of their points of resemblance. But they were alike with a difference—discord which perhaps the more closely cemented their union,—

"Fletcher's keen treble and deep Beaumont's base."

Beaumont, though not himself a landed proprietor, was the descendant of two successive owners of Grace-dieu in Leicestershire, and brother of a third. He was "smit with the love of song," and of the company at the Mermaid, but he had his seasons of retirement from theatrical and club life, and saw

the oaks wave and the deer course over the lawns
of his birthplace.   He married, too, an heiress —
" Ursula, daughter and coheir of Henry Isley, of
Sundridge, in Kent."   Now, as Pompey says, " I
hope here be truths;" and they tend to show that
if Beaumont improved his means by writing for the
stage, he was at least not driven by poverty to authorship.   He was a member of the Inner Temple,
and, like so many Templars then and since, a wit
also—a combination seldom so favourable to law as
to poetry, in spite of the recent example of Mr. Justice Talfourd to the contrary.   Fletcher's case was
probably very different.   Fortune at first seemed to
smile propitious on his birth.   Queen Elizabeth took
a fancy to the cut of his father's beard, and preferred
him with almost railway speed from a prebendary and
a royal chaplaincy to the deanery of Peterborough—
from the deanery of Peterborough, in the course of
five years, to the sees of Bristol, Worcester, and London.   Bishop Fletcher was as great a pluralist as the
Dragon of Wantley, who "devoured churches like geese
and turkeys," and, from his procedure touching the
see of London, we fear he was somewhat simoniacal.
He had a worse fault than simony; " he was peevish,
and given to prayer" at unseasonable times, for he was
the very Dean Fletcher who troubled the dying moments of the Queen of Scots with dissuasions from
Popery.   At any rate he was a prosperous gentleman;
" loved to ride the great horse," says Fuller, " and was

condemned for very proud by such as knew him not."
He might perhaps, but for one false step, have been
his Grace of Canterbury. But he married a second
time, and bade a short adieu to all his greatness. Dr.
Primrose himself was not a more zealous monogamist
than Queen Elizabeth. She hardly brooked, as Bishop
Grindal found to his cost, " speech of marriage " in
clergymen. However, Bishop Fletcher's well-trimmed
beard and courtly demeanour brought him ere long
into favour again: he was promised a royal visit, "fitted
up his hall at Fulham" in readiness, and, perhaps,
might have thriven as well as ever but for an untowardly
accident. He died—some said of grief at her Majesty's
displeasure, others "of taking too much tobacco." Un-
certain it must ever remain whether he used common
shag or the finest Virginia, but certain it is that he
left as many children and as little money as if, instead
of his pluralities, he had been all his life a curate.
During his rapid preferments he had been at great
charges for induction-fees and first-fruits, and did not
live to reimburse himself by an episcopal harvest of
rents and fines. Had the Bishop's life been spared,
the world might have had one dramatist less, for John
Fletcher was already at Bene't College, and in a few
years more might have been safely niched in a stall;
and, with Abbot or Andrewes in place of Jonson for
his model, have drawn graver audiences than at Black-
friars or the Globe. But henceforth he must live by
his wits. In that age, all popular literature centred

in the stage. The theatre was at once the newspaper, the review, the magazine, and the novel of the seventeenth century. We then imported romances and invented plays, a process which is now nearly inverted. The stage was not indeed a high-road to fortune—Shakespeare and Alleyne being among the few who put, or at least kept, money in their purses; but for talents of any mark or likelihood, it was almost a sure road to fame. Rowley, a rugged versifier, and, "in respect of a fine workman," one of the drama's journeymen, is better remembered than many a popular preacher of his day; for not even Lamb could have made attractive "Specimens of Divines." And besides the pulpit and the stage they were few avenues in that age to literary renown. History was locked up in folios, debates were unreported, and the art and mystery of reviewing was undiscovered. The number and fertility of playwrights was unprecedented and unsurpassed. The novelists of the nineteenth century are not ten times as numerous as the dramatic writers in Fletcher's age; and if the number of readers *now* and *then* be considered, the proportion of playwrights was even greater. We possess a portion only of the printed dramas; the fire of London; servants as careless as Mr. Warburton's; or politic Diets of Worms, have thinned their ranks. A much larger portion of acted plays was never sent to press, but remained in manuscript among the managers' properties. Not a third of the Sibylline books has come down to us.

Into this broad and swelling stream Beaumont
and his colleague cast their intellectual fortunes, and
Fletcher probably staked his whole venture in life.
To Beaumont tradition, if not express testimony, has
assigned superior judgment. From his easier fortunes he may have been less enterprising and hasty
in composition than his friend. Of Fletcher's poverty we have indeed no direct evidence, and in some
verses prefixed by him to the 'Faithful Shepherdess'
we have something like a denial of its pressure.
Mr. Darley asks if Bishop Fletcher, who remembered
a *college*, would have forgotten a *son* in his will?
But Bishop Fletcher's bequests resembled Diego's
in his son's 'Spanish Curate.' His executors must
have asked, "Where shall we find these sums?"
"The truth is," says Mr. Dyce, "none of Fletcher's
biographers were aware of the poverty in which his
father died." The question would be immaterial
were it not calculated to explain the haste and negligence which many of these dramas betray. A
writer who produced thirty-one plays, with little occasional help, in eleven years; who lived in good
society, and not with the most prudent and thrifty
associates, had probably an urgent motive "to coin
his brain or drop its sweat for drachmas." His
verses prefixed to the 'Honest Man's Fortune' prove,
however, that Fletcher was rather elevated than de-
pressed by his circumstances. His mind to him a
kingdom was. They read like Milton's protestations

D

of his integrity and independence, like Wordsworth's 'Happy Warrior.'

The respective shares of Beaumont and Fletcher in the dramas which bear their joint names is an insoluble problem. It is an interesting one only because their plays betray at times the influence of opposite schools, and because its solution might show how much they owed to Jonson and how much to Shakespeare. Beaumont was bred up at the feet of that dramatic Gamaliel, Ben Jonson, who understood "the theorique" of his art better than the "practique;" Fletcher is termed by Dryden "a limb of Shakespeare." So long as it was the fashion to regard Shakespeare as a "wild, irregular genius," Beaumont's superior judiciousness might seem to indicate the Jonsonian discipline. But now that the consummate art of Shakespeare is as universally recognized as his transcendent powers, Beaumont's reputation for judgment, even if it rested on surer foundations, will not avail us. When however we compare the plays which Fletcher wrote singly with those which he wrote conjointly, the theory that

"Beaumont's judgment check'd what Fletcher writ,"

must depart into the lumber-room of respectable fallacies, where already is reposing Cromwell's damnation to everlasting fame, and whither Bacon's meanness will probably soon follow. For it is universally admitted that the 'Woman-Hater,' was produced by Fletcher before his literary partnership with

Beaumont began; and the two prominent characters in this comedy, Gondarino and Lazarillo, are constructed on the Jonsonian model of analyzing, or rather running down, an odd fantastic humour. Fletcher therefore was as much a disciple of Jonson as his colleague. On the other hand, the plays ascribed to both partners, the tragedies especially, are neither more nor less judicious than those which Fletcher produced after Beaumont's decease. Nay, if Mr. Darley be right in attributing "to Beaumont chiefly" the 'Knight of the Burning Pestle,' his wit would seem to have been the more luxuriant of the two; for in none of the fifty-two dramas is there such exuberance of fancy, or such riotous animal spirits. Nothing is more deceptive than internal evidence in deciding questions of doubtful authorship, where the disputed work is not a forgery. It required only the common instincts of the pit and gallery to detect Ireland's 'Vortigern;' and none but the shallowest scholars, and blinded by party zeal to boot, would have maintained the genuineness of the 'Epistles of Phalaris.' But the case is very different when a controversy arises whether the 'Rhesus' or 'Iphigenia at Tauris' were written by Euripides, or whether they proceeded from the Sophoclean school. Here internal evidence is a very Will-o'-the-wisp, a preconception in the mind of B. of what A. must have written, B. not being at all in A.'s secrets, but probably separated from him by "sounding seas" and sundry generations.

We are not disposed to put much faith in commenda-
tory verses, having had some experience in testimonials
to character. Both are alike granted by friendly zeal
or good-natured indolence. But we incline to think
that the author of a contemporary eulogy on Fletcher
has stated the question of his literary partnership
with Beaumont more fully and fairly than any subse-
quent commentator or critic :—

> "Some think your wits of two complexions framed,
> That one the sock, th' other the buskin claimed :
> That should the stage embattle all its force,
> Fletcher would lead the foot, Beaumont the horse :
> But you were both for both, not semi-wits :
> Each piece is wholly two, yet never splits ;
> Ye are not two faculties and one soul still,
> He th' understanding, thou the quick free-will ;
> But, as two voices in one song embrace,
> Fletcher's keen treble and deep Beaumont's bass,
> Two, full, congenial souls ; still both prevailed ;
> His Muse and thine were quartered, not impaled :
> Both brought your ingots, both toiled at the mint,
> Beat, melted, sifted till no dross stuck in't.
> Then in each other's scales weighed every grain,
> Then smoothed and burnished, then weighed all again ;
> Stampt both your names upon't at one bold hit,
> Then, then 't was coin as well as bullion-wit."

The scanty personal records of dramatic poets may
sometimes be illustrated or supplied by the traces of
contemporary events impressed upon their writings.
As the abstracts and brief chronicles of their time,
they may be supposed to have watched with no in-
curious eye the heavings and flashings of the great
world-stream that circled their round of life, to have

been moved by it to lyrical responses, to have represented it in passionate symbols and similitudes. Mr. C. Knight, in his 'Shakespeare: a Biography,' amid much fanciful and some valuable matter, has shown that the myriad-minded bard attentively regarded the movements of his age, and sometimes embodied what was passing around him in everlasting forms and colours. Beaumont and Fletcher exhibit fewer marks of sympathy with the world's business and mutations than Shakespeare, or even Jonson and Massinger. They appear to have moved between the stage and the closet, the Club and the Court alone. We know, on unquestionable authority, that they bore a prominent part in the *symposia* at the 'Mermaid,' and were sprung from fathers, one at least of whom watched anxiously the smiles of the Sovereign and the intrigues of the palace. But, for any tokens to the contrary, the brother-dramatists cared more for Philip Henslowe's acceptance of their plays than for "what the Swede intended or what the French." The reign of James was indeed far less favourable than that of Elizabeth had been for poetic sympathy with public events: it was the most peaceful which England had hitherto enjoyed. Notwithstanding the ghastly abortion of the Gunpowder Plot, the dark tragedy of Overbury, the expectations and the catastrophe of Raleigh's expedition, and the Protestant interest in the Palatinate War, it afforded few of those scenes,

"Sad, high, and working full of state and woe,"

which filled and made memorable the sway of the
Maiden Queen. There was no life-long tragedy, like
that of the Queen of Scots; no stern and solemn
pause of preparation, like that which awaited the Ar-
mada; no universal shout of jubilee over the fallen,
like that which hailed its wreck; no bonfires for the
burning of Cadiz; no welcome of Drake from victory
and pillage on the Spanish Main. The grave splendour of Elizabeth was exchanged for slovenly extravagance: the sceptre had become a pedant's ferula.
Bacon was indeed the Chancellor; but Oxford, and
Sidney, and the greater Cecil, had left no inheritors of
their chivalry or their wisdom. A sullen gloom was
settling on the national mind. The cloud of Puritan-
ism, lately no bigger than a man's hand, lay billowy
on the horizon; the martial genius of the people was
thwarted by an irresolute and inglorious Sovereign,
or exasperated by incapable leaders and ill-concerted
enterprises. Parliaments were grown jealous of monarchy, and monarchy distrusted parliaments. Queen
Elizabeth had ever wisely distinguished between her
counsellors and her courtiers: the one ministered to
the strength, the others to the splendour of the realm.
James hearkened to favourites, and placed reliance
in spies; created a mushroom nobility, and sent away
malcontent the Cliffords, Howards, and De Veres.
The Plantagenets and Tudors, however arbitrary at
times, were English Sovereigns in heart. The Stuarts
looked abroad for models of kingcraft, and repined at

their limitary right-divine. They aspired to the license
of the Tuileries and the stately ceremonial of the Es-
curial. But the feeling of the nation reverted to its
ancestral hostility with the one, and to its recent con-
tact with the other. Religious earnestness sanctioned
political dread; and the King and courtiers alone had
forgotten the day of St. Bartholomew and "the sad
intelligencing tyrant who mischieved the world with
his mines of Ophir." The Court and the people were
entering upon a fierce antagonism; and the drama, if
it alluded at all to current events, spoke with bated
breath and in a bondman's key. But although
many signs of the times are not legible in Beaumont
and Fletcher, they were not altogether unimpressed
by them. There is a difference between the tone of
their sentiments, whether comic or heroic, and that
of the manlier drama of Elizabeth. There is a moral
decadence, an imaginative decay. The hues of autumn
have begun to streak the poetic foliage; the line of
the horizon is less clear; the coherence and intertex-
ture of form and colour are less tenacious and less
genial. The irony of Sophocles and Shakespeare regards man struggling impotently with circumstance,
and is the imaginative expression of the strife between Fate and Free-will; the irony of Beaumont
and Fletcher is the utterance of the satirist on men
and manners. The former is consistent with the loftiest
passion and the deepest pathos; the latter is conversant only with the superficial emotions and conven-

tional forms of life. The one betrays a spirit at variance with itself, and perplexed in the extreme by
the enigma of life: it is the spirit of Jaques, Timon,
and Hamlet. The other indicates a temper which
contemplates and derides the phenomena of society,
without attempting to solve them by any higher law
of reconcilement: it is the temper of Lucian, Mon-
taigne, and Voltaire. We do not rise from the perusal
of Beaumont and Fletcher much the happier or the
wiser. They deal too much with the merely concrete
and conventional to be genuinely humorous or earnest.
Their flashes of wit and fancy, their crowded incidents
and startling contrasts, even the voluptuous music of
their verse, are things of sense and of the scene, not
echoes from the fontal deeps of humanity. Their
works may enliven or soothe a vacant hour; but they
are not for seasons when the mind would enter into
its secret chambers and commune with the verities
of sadness or mirth. "Beaumont and Fletcher,"
Schlegel well remarks, "were men of the most distinguished talents: they scarcely wanted anything
more than a profounder seriousness of mind, and
that artistic sagacity which everywhere observes a due
measure, to rank beside the greatest dramatic poets
of all nations. But with them poetry was not an
inward devotion of the feelings and imagination, but
a means to obtain brilliant results."

Coleridge's remarks upon the brother dramatists
are for the most part as strictly just as they are acute

and ingenious. He is, indeed, one of the best commentators on these poets, both in what he has written and in what he has suggested, and he was the first who examined their metrical system critically. We think however that he has rather overstated his charge against them of "exuberant loyalty." Their kings are, indeed, as self-willed and licentious as any Greek or Italian despots on record, and their courtiers as servile and supple as Damocles himself. Yet the general impression on reading these dramas is not favourable to loyalty; and their treatment of Court favourites seems to point shrewdly at their own times and real persons. In the plays of Beaumont and Fletcher we step from the precincts of a legal monarchy into those of arrogant and unveiled despotism. It is needless to cite examples when almost any one of Mr. Dyce's eleven volumes will furnish them. Wherever the action of tragedy or the graver cast of comedy turns upon the will and pleasure of the scenic King, Duke, or Count, the virtuous suffer unreasonably, and female purity and manly honour are exposed to extravagant trials. This may be partly owing to Spanish originals, but is also a reflection of contemporary manners. The hot and peremptory Elizabeth exacted obedience but not servility, and was often better pleased with a frank reply than with a cunning compliment. The pedantic and equally arbitrary James delighted in the homage of his courtiers, because it exemplified the theory of his 'Basilicon Doron,' or soothed his suspicions of his own irresolute and unkingly temper. The king's favourite is a very frequent character with Beaumont and Fletcher. The satire is indeed veiled, but is not the less pungent and significant. In the days of Somerset and Buckingham, Boroskie in the 'Loyal Subject' is styled "a malicious, seducing counsellor to the Duke." Latorch, in the 'Bloody Brother,' is quaintly called "Rollo's earwig;" and in the 'Wife for a Month' and 'Beggar's Bush' Sorano and Heinskirk are the usurper's "wicked instruments." More license than this was not likely to be allowed to his Majesty's servants. At a later day, and under very different circumstances, politics were brought openly upon the stage. Bolingbroke and the Duchess of Marlborough vied with each other in applauding the *Whig* Addison's 'Cato,' and the country party cheered the hits at Sir Robert Walpole in the 'Beggar's Opera.' Beaumont and Fletcher were, for their age, free-spoken, and implied more than they thought it politic to set down. We do not find, indeed, that their ears were ever endangered like Ben Jonson's for his share in 'Eastward Ho,' or that they ever received a hint from the Star Chamber that the King or Buckingham were offended.

Fletcher himself probably regarded with indifference his rapidity of composition and the consequent imperfection of many of his plays. He knew well what suited the players and pleased the public, and had probably no deeper artistic yearnings. He had in-

deed little of that earnest sympathy with his characters which enforced Shakespeare to infuse his own
lyrical sensations and self-questionings into his *dramatis personæ*. He had even less of that artistic purpose and prescience which brooded over Göthe in his
'Faust' and 'Iphigenia.' He was rather eloquent than
impassioned; rather ingenious than inventive; and
more studious of effect than of consistency or even
probability. It may however in some measure explain, or at least palliate, the feeble coherence or unnatural transitions in his plays, if we remember that
in Fletcher's time there were no *after-pieces* in the
modern sense of the term; for the *jigs* which followed
the play were such ballets as we may see at this day
in booths at country wakes. In the modern theatre
we require at least two pieces to satisfy our dramatic
appetites. Our ancestors were less devious in their
longings, or more frugal of their time. Our elder
drama was accompanied by neither farce nor melodrama, neither opera nor spectacle. The performance
rarely exceeded two hours; and into this period were
to be compressed all possible variety and excitement.
The absence of scenery, and the scantiness of appointments, were compensated by a rich wardrobe and rapid
turns in the plot. It is not fair therefore to try such
pieces as the 'Island Princess,' the 'Sea Voyage,' or the
'Coxcomb,' by a strict standard of dramatic propriety:
they belong rather to the staple attractions of the
Adelphi, to the 'Victorines' and 'Green Bushes.' They

were as stimulant and attractive as melodrama, and much more poetical.

Much discussion has been raised as to the quality of Fletcher's genteel comedy. For while it is agreed that he was the precursor of Wycherley, Congreve, and Farquhar, it is disputed whether he surpassed or was inferior to Shakespeare in the portraiture of gentlemen. Dryden has affirmed that "Shakespeare wrote better as between man and man; Fletcher as between man and woman." To this assertion Mr. Hallam furnishes the very pertinent reply, that "this will be granted when he shall be shown to have excelled Ferdinand and Miranda, or Posthumus and Imogen." But both Mr. Hallam and Coleridge have suggested that, from their higher station in society, Beaumont and Fletcher represent the phrase and manners of the more polished circles more truly than their great contemporary. We are tempted to turn Mr. Hallam's words against himself, and say this may be granted when the Don Johns, Don Felixes, and Rutilios, of these dramatists, shall be shown to have excelled in conversation Orlando in Ardennes, Benedick at Messina, and Cassio in Cyprus. The difference, we apprehend, may be thus stated :—We do not go quite so far as Mr. Darley, who thinks Beaumont and Fletcher's gentlemen, "fancy men" or bucks; but we suggest, upon the evidence of their banter and their love-making, that they copied more faithfully than Shakespeare the language of the Court and the

Mall. "To be like the Court was a playe's praise." But James's favourites, who set the fashion, were neither men of the highest birth nor the most decorous manners. James himself was not more choice in his words than gainly in his person; and neither Carr nor Villiers were Hattons or Chesterfields. Even the Puritans admitted that Charles's Court was more decent than his father's; and that staunch but candid Loyalist, Sir Philip Warwick, pronounced Cromwell's levees "to be greatly more choice and solemne" than his predecessor's. It was from the earlier and coarser of these originals that Fletcher copied his gentlemen. Shakespeare's models, when he drew from actual life, were the statelier manners of "great Eliza's golden prime." But there is a further distinction. Not only were the Benedicks and Orlandos—creatures partly of earth and partly of fancy —drawn from a more catholic pattern than court fashions could supply, but James's Court by no means absorbed the gentlemen of the realm. The fathers of Hyde, Twysden, Lucy Hutchinson, and Falkland, were country gentlemen, and although they occasionally attended levees, or even were suitors for sinecures, lived much on their estates, and were rather brow-beaten than caressed by the modern Solomon and "Babie Charles." It may be granted, then, that Fletcher caught the trick and passing fashion of the spruce gamesters and curled darlings of his age: but it does not follow that he represented better the general traits and demeanour of the English gentleman.

That Fletcher "wrote better as between man and woman than Shakespeare," is an opinion already disposed of by Mr. Hallam. We approach with more diffidence the following remark of Charles Lamb. He has pronounced Ordella, in 'Thierry and Theodoret,' "the most perfect idea of the female heroic character, next to Calantha in the 'Broken Heart' of Ford." Is this a paradox, or a heresy of the most genial and orthodox of dramatic commentators? Had he, when he wrote, a momentary oblivion of Cordelia, of Imogen, and of Isabella? Does Ordella,⸴like these, dwell in the memory? Is *she* among our visions? Is *she* "remembered in our orisons"? Mr. Dyce observes more justly, that "Brunhalt and Ordella present one of those violent contrasts which our authors loved to exhibit; and though both characters are strained very far beyond the truth of nature, there is unquestionably much strong painting in the fiendish wickedness of the former, and many beautiful touches in the angelic purity of the latter." Mr. Darley has in one sentence described very happily the general character of Beaumont and Fletcher's female portraitures. "They seem to have caught one deep truth of nature,—their women are either far more angelical or diabolical than their men." Another remark of Lamb's, however, is full of significance. He suggests that the performance of women's parts by boys led to the frequent introduc-

tion of the page upon the scene—the page being generally a disguised damsel in quest of a faithless or un-
conscious lover. "Our ancestors," he adds, "seem
to have been wonderfully delighted with these trans-
formations of sex. What an odd double confusion it
must have made to see a boy play a woman playing a
man! one cannot disentangle the perplexity without
some violence to the imagination." An apology was
made by a stage-manager to Charles II. for keeping
his Majesty waiting—"The Queen was shaving." The
practice however was productive of more than scenic
ambiguity. It contributed to render both the poet's
and the actor's delineation of women coarser. Even
Shakespeare sometimes slides into the temptation which
this *epicenism* presents to unlicensed wit. But where
Shakespeare merely stumbled, his contemporaries fell;
and none fell lower at times than Fletcher. The appearance of ladies in male attire had indeed become
so common that Queen Elizabeth declined, on *political* grounds only, Sir Andrew Melville's proposal to
escort her Majesty in a page's dress to Scotland, that
in this disguise she might see, unseen herself, her
beautiful rival, Mary Stuart. Henrietta and her ladies
of honour performed, not only "boy Cleopatras" and
Bellarios, but in the "Masques at Court," Cupid,
Zephyrus, and Iris, in very classical and scanty costume. Shakespeare rarely employs this scenic device.
In Julia and Portia it takes the form of a pleasant
freak: Viola and Imogen resort to it as the readiest

escape from their dilemmas; but in Fletcher's comedies the boy-woman is repeated *ad nauseam*. It is
adopted in his best plays, it is lavished on his worst;
and in 'Love's Pilgrimage' alone we have no fewer than
three ladies thus disguised. And even where the page
is not introduced, the knowledge that a handsome
stripling was before them tended to reconcile the audience to the license of Lælia, Bacha, and Hippolyta.
Dryden, who surpasses Fletcher in indecency, had not
even his excuse for it. Women-actors came in with
the Restoration; and Kynaston, who was afterwards
celebrated for his demeanour in kings and soldans,
had been equally famous in his youth for his *feminine*
impersonations.

We are not disposed in all cases to admit Mr. Dyce's
verdicts on particular plays. He seems to us hardly
fair to Fletcher's later dramas, and to have adopted
rather too implicitly the opinions of preceding critics
upon the earlier ones. The 'Maid's Tragedy' is a favourite with editors; and we have some diffidence in
questioning the merits of a play which has been repro-
duced on the stage by such competent judges as Mr.
Sheridan Knowles and Mr. Macready. But we think
this one of the plays which has "been to the fair of
good names and bought a reasonable commodity of
them." It has indeed striking stage-effects and passages of brilliant declamation. But, with the exception of Aspasia, a poetic rather than a dramatic creation, its characters are uninteresting and even heart-

less. Melanthius is not a better stage soldier than
Pierre in 'Venice Preserved.' Nay, Pierre has public
wrongs to avenge, while Melanthius's grief, although
profound, is selfish. The King is an ordinary despot
of the Italian novel; and Amintor, who at first offends
us by his fickleness in love, finally disgusts us by a
ceremonious and fantastic loyalty, utterly dispropor-
tioned to the wrong he has undergone. Evadne claims
about as much sympathy as Milnwood in 'George
Barnwell.' Her sin is rank; her repentance is worse.
The character may have been barely tolerable when
acted by a boy: performed by women it is unendurable.

On the other hand, we think Mr. Dyce has under-
valued 'The Knight of Malta.' "This tragi-comedy,"
he says, "with a rambling plot and very few characters
which are vigorously delineated, has some highly dramatic and interesting scenes, and a profusion of beautiful writing." There are in it only nine male and
three female characters of any prominence—a short
allowance for our group-loving ancestors. Yet of
these twelve personages, Miranda, Gomera, and Montferrat are clearly defined and opposed; and their
female correlates, Oriana, Zanthia, and Lucilla, have,
for our dramatists, unusual variety and precision. We
are surprised that no manager has thought of reviving
'The Knight of Malta.' The plot would improve by
the necessary retrenchments; modern scenery would
set off to advantage the Chapter and Procession of
the Knights at Valetta, and Montferrat be a part not

unworthy of Macready himself. We recommend this
and some of the less popular of Fletcher's plays to the
attention of Mr. R. H. Horne, who has so skilfully
adapted the ' Honest Man's Fortune' to the modern
stage. No art in the poet, nor accomplishment in
the performers, will again restore 'A King and No
King,' ' Philaster,' or ' The Faithful Shepherdess' to
the répertoire of acting plays. But in proportion as
Fletcher departed from the schools of Shakespeare and
Jonson, he acquired a lower but more natural tone,
and, with less ambition, was really more successful.
He was an artist of the second order, constrained to
unnatural and spasmodical movements while he remained in the higher regions of art, but moving
gracefully and spontaneously when he descended to
the lower.

We had purposed a few words on the poetry of
Fletcher apart from the drama, on his metrical system
which Mr. Darley has somewhat misrepresented, and
on their relation to the literature of fiction generally.
But our space is exhausted; and it only remains for
us once more to acknowledge our obligations to Mr.
Dyce for his critical and editorial labours on these
Dioscuri of the English stage.

PLAYS AND THEIR PROVIDERS.*

IF the records of the stage speak truth, they are among the most melancholy of chronicles, since, according to them, acting is always declining and the theatres on the verge of insolvency. It is scarcely possible to conceive, if we credit these narratives, how any class of mortals can embrace so disastrous a profession, or how any man, not being a proven lunatic, should of his own accord undergo the drudgery and disappointments of managership. From Colley Cibber to Mr. Alfred Bunn, the annals of the theatre are one long Jeremiad of vexations from without and from within; so that we are led to think that, in comparison with the sceptre of the green-room, the treadmill must be a pleasant recreation, and Norfolk Island a comfortable retreat.

Yet doubtless such cares must have their attendant consolations; for otherwise it could not be that, "like leaves on trees," the generations of actors and managers should succeed one another, and even increase

* Reprinted from 'Fraser's Magazine,' September 1853.

and multiply, in the regions of perpetual embarrassment. Who ever yet found an actor willing to quit
the stage, or, having quitted it, not casting a longing,
lingering look behind? And even as the stoutest
protectionists continue to buy and hire land, although
they affirm that land and loss are become convertible
terms, so is it common for an actor who has provi-
dently saved money, as improvidently to turn manager and lose it. We are unable to reconcile these
contradictions, and are driven to the conclusion that
the theatrical world, unlike the real world, is composed of self-devoted persons who immolate themselves on the altars of public entertainment.

But are the chronicles true?—is it indeed the fact
that actors, like certain doomed races of mankind,
are always degenerating, and that management and
insolvency are inseparable? May not the premises
on which these suppositions rest be false; or, if partially true, may not the circumstances of decline and
embarrassment be traced to other than the commonly
assigned causes? It appears from a useful little book
now before us—an attempt at theatrical statistics
which deserves encouragement*—that during the
year 1852 no less than twenty-seven theatres and
saloons opened their doors to the public within the
boundaries of London, Westminster, and Southwark;
and that no fewer than two hundred and twenty theatrical entertainments were produced at them, "for

---

* 'Dramatic Register' for 1852.

the first time." This account implies, though it does
not expressly state, that many hundred persons,
during that period, found it worth their while to devote their time and their intellects to pursuits which
the chroniclers of the stage represent as in the last
degree vexatious and unremunerative. On the other
hand, and in direct opposition to the said chroniclers,
the daily and weekly bills of performance vie with
one another, and exhaust language for superlatives
expressive of "unbounded success," "rapturous applause," and "numbers numberless" of spectators.
The truth of the matter is indeed, like Samson's
riddle, "hard to hit—though one should three days
musing sit."

For our parts, we believe neither the prophets who
prophesy smooth things, nor those who run up and
down, crying, "Woe, and threefold woe;" neither that
acting is always deteriorating, nor that managers are
for ever on the brink of insolvency. We are however
persuaded that the one might become more attractive
by rejecting a good many foolish stage traditions, and
by a different system of discipline; and that the others
increase the risks of a necessarily hazardous speculation by attempts beyond the power of the stage to
realize, and by an insane rivalry of one another. We
will first glance at the difficulties incident to managers.

These have doubtless been increased by the greater
number of theatres. We believe that the Act of

William IV., 1833, abolishing or considerably modi-
fying the old limitations of the patent theatres, was a
measure called for by the exigencies of the case and
the increasing population of the Metropolis. Yet it
is in vain to deny that the extended privileges have
operated, in some respects, unfavourably upon the
histrionic art. With twenty-seven theatres of more
or less importance, open nearly at the same time, it
has become next to impossible for a manager to col-
lect, or if collected to keep long together, an efficient
troupe of performers. The second-rate actor of a
West-end theatre, especially if he excels in " Hercles'
vein," is the "magnus Apollo" of a city establishment, and by merely crossing "the bridges" earns
golden opinions, and an advanced salary to boot.
His praises indeed are not sung in the columns of
the 'Times' or 'Morning Chronicle,' but his pudding
is sure, and he is probably not nice as to the discrimination of his audiences. But from this it results,
not only that the lucky emigrant to the east has less
urgent motives to study the details of his art, and to
raise himself by just gradations in his profession, but
also that his duties at a superior theatre devolve,
through his absence, upon still less competent performers than himself, and, both by what it loses and
what it keeps, the general character of the *troupe* is
impaired. And even in the case of better performers
than the one we have supposed, the number of theatres of a higher order is adverse to the stability of a

company, unless the manager buys his monopoly at a
heavy pecuniary sacrifice. At the patent theatres the
same company played for years together, in the winter
at Covent Garden or Drury Lane, in the summer
season at the Haymarket, or at most varied their engagements by "starring it" in the country. They
thus acquired both a distinctive position in their respective circles, and a corporate interest in the company generally. Each, in short, became a part of a
well-organized whole. Even to actors of the first
order this was no inconsiderable advantage. It was
a kind of regimental discipline, or rather such. a
training as two "elevens" at cricket gain by playing
customarily on the same ground. To inferior performers, again, it was a decided benefit to perform
frequently with the acknowledged masters of their
art. Whereas under the present system there is no
such principle of collision; an actor flits from the
Haymarket to the Adelphi, from the Adelphi to the
Olympic theatres without attaching himself to any
one of them. By frequency of change the general
discipline is slackened; and managers, vexed with
the uncertainty of their *troupes,* come to regard their
scenery and wardrobe as the only permanent forces of
their establishment.

Another source of managerial difficulty in collect-
ing a company arises from the circumstance that provincial theatres have nearly ceased to be the nurseries
of the metropolitan stage. In the provinces, for a

theatre to pay the expenses of keeping it open is now almost as great a prodigy as if an ox should speak. The rural frequenters of the playhouse, whom a few hours and a few shillings will convey to the Strand, think scorn of the performances that contented their simpler and less locomotive sires. Even in Race or Assize weeks the Stewards' and Sheriffs' "bespeaks" do not half fill the boxes. The country manager consequently has neither the means nor a motive for training or seeking out histrionic talents; and if his company should possess a performer better than ordinary, the world of London is all before him where to choose. In the days of the patent theatres he would have been a hardy *débutant,* and most probably a luckless one, who had ventured to meet a metropolitan audience before he established his provincial character at Bath, Norwich, or York. At one or other of those cities, and sometimes in all three, he served his apprenticeship; at York especially, under the well-known Tate Wilkinson, the aspirant was sure to receive a sound education in his art, somewhat roughly administered. Whereas now, under the regimen of theatrical free-trade, the city theatres have taken the place of the provincial, and the *terra incognita* of Shoreditch or Whitechapel intercepts many a recruit who would otherwise have been cleaving with horrid shout the general ear at Plymouth or Southampton. This however is but a poor substitute for the more regular discipline of an established pro-

vincial theatre, for although the "legitimate drama"
(Shakespeare included) is much encouraged by the
men of the cast, as yet no Roscius has "stepped westward" from those regions, nor indeed is the style of
acting favoured there likely to recruit more westerly
theatres with many efficient members.

Doubtless among the stock-pieces in vogue fifty
years ago there were many which the present age
would no longer endure, and which have been most
rightfully consigned to that valley of dust and dry
bones, the library of the theatre.   Our grandsires
were contented and even edified by performances
which we, accustomed to more stimulating species of
literature, account utterly stale, flat, and unprofitable.
Another generation may very possibly designate the
bulk of our present dramatic compositions by even
harsher names.   But let them look to that matter;
we are now neither absolving nor condemning. Many
however of these flat and unprofitable stock-pieces, as
we now esteem them, are really better adapted to the
conditions of histrionic art than the broader horrors
and humours of the present stage.   They attempted,
in the first place, no rivalry with literature—as literary productions, indeed, they are for the most part
below contempt—and by abstaining from such competition, their authors proved themselves wiser in their
generation than many of their successors; for though
the spheres of the drama and literature may occasionally touch, they can never coincide without respective

E

forfeiture of their proper natures. In some respects, indeed, the literature of the day acts unfavourably upon the theatres.

We can take tea and scandal, or sup full with horrors at home, through the medium of our novelists, without exposing ourselves to the disasters of heated rooms, narrow benches, crowds, or unjust cabmen. But these domestic and untroubled delights impose upon authors, actors, and managers a necessity for providing us, if they would live by their callings, with something yet more stimulating abroad. We Englishmen are often twitted with being an uninventive people; and assuredly, though we occasionally produce a startling murder, yet in devising stage horrors, or in conceiving intricate yet cunningly evolved plots, we come very far behind our neighbours in France. "To convey"—as the wise call it —a drama from Paris, is now, with a few striking exceptions, our only practice. We notice it however on this occasion, merely to remark upon its relations to acting. We admit the frequent excellence of the plots so conveyed; yet we are persuaded that they both lose considerably by the transfer, and impose new burdens on the actors. They lose by the transfer, because our ways are not as their ways, our manners and morals—be they better or worse is not now the question—are not French manners and morals; and, accordingly, the actor can no longer copy from the life which he sees, but is constrained to transcribe a

model with which he is unacquainted. Neither is
our language—so superior in many higher respects—
adapted to the conversational tone of French comedy;
and, therefore, in most of the adoptions, while the
plot remains nearly intact, the lightness and grace of
the dialogue is, in many cases, sacrificed. As far
as regards the diction alone, we succeed better with
the French melodrama. Yet, even in this case, the
actor is forced into undue exaggeration, in order that
his impersonation may not sink below the unnatural
situations or terrors of the scenes. In the older
farces—those veterans which sufficed our simpler ancestors—the humour was, at least, English; and in
the older tragedies, the part generally demanded some
study from the performer. In the modern farce and
melodrama, the actor has little more to do than to
accommodate his idiosyncrasy to the part. It would
be useless for him to study actual life for the purpose
of representing sentiments or situations that occur
only in the teeming brains of the writers.

It would be easy for us to mention the names of
English writers for the stage to whose productions
none of these objections will apply, and English
actors who, in the midst of improbabilities and extravagances, retain the love of their art, and model themselves upon the realities of life. But our censure,
such as it is, refers exclusively to the general aspect
and conditions of the stage at the present moment, to
the taste which the public at once fosters and imbibes,

and to the causes which, in our opinion, render the provinces of both managers and actors peculiarly difficult and embarrassing. We refrain therefore equally from blame or praise of individuals. The faults we note are simply those of the system.

When Garrick, after much justifiable coyness and reluctance on his part, produced, at great expense, and, as it proved, with very indifferent success, Glover's stupid tragedy of 'Agis,' the chorus were robed in surplices, and looked like the choristers of a cathedral. Horace Walpole detected the absurdity, but in matters of art and costume he stood almost alone in his age. Had the play been endurable, the surplices would have been deemed orthodox. We have passed to the opposite extreme, and represent the drama of Elizabeth and Charles with all the anxious precision of an archæological society. We apply to Shakespeare and his contemporaries the zeal for correctness of accessories which our shrewd satirist has noted in the collectors of coins:

> " With sharpened sight pale antiquaries pore,
> The inscription value, but the *rust* adore."

The passion, the poetry, the plot of 'King John' and 'Macbeth' will not now fill pit or boxes, unless the manager lavishes a fortune on pictures of high Dunsinane, or on coats of mail and kilts such as were actually worn by the Earls and Thanes of the English and Scottish Courts. We write this with all honour to the enterprising manager who has set these dramas

on the stage so gorgeously and accurately accoutred.
Yet we take leave to doubt whether, by this excess
of decoration, new difficulties be not imposed on the
actor; whether, indeed, the substance of the drama
has not become less important than its accessories.
In representations of the highest tragedy or comedy,
the poet himself should, in our opinion, occupy the
first place; to him the actor is, or should be, wholly
subservient.   Again, the actor, if he be one really
capable of embodying the highest moods of passion,
should be independent of the antiquary and robe-
maker; and although we would not send the representative of Macbeth back to the modern uniform
in which Garrick played, we would not regard archæological precision of garb as an indispensable condition of success in the character.   We do not echo
the objection which we have frequently heard, that
the upholsterer is called in to veil the defects of the
actor; but we would submit that theatrical decoration has its limits, and that recently there has been a
tendency to overstep them.   The conditions of scenic
effect are, it appears to us, not difficult to define.
They are the framework of the picture, not the picture itself. So much then of pictorial art—and under
this head we include costume—as is really needed for
illustration, is a legitimate adjunct. We do not think
that exact copies of the swords, helmets, and mantles
of any given period are required for proper dramatic
effects. We do not attach much importance to scenes

representing the real localities of the dramatic action.
It is enough that time and place be not confounded
by anachronisms. The object of pictorial illustrations
on the stage, is not so much the historical as the poetical element of the drama. We would not, were it possible, return to a green-baize curtain, labelled "This
is a street in Padua," or "This is the Wood of Ardennes;" neither would we insist upon a representation of the actual street or the actual wood. It is
sufficient that there be no disharmony; it is enough
that the adjuncts be as local as the poetry of the
particular drama. Above all things, an artistic sense
of the beautiful should preside and predominate over
scenical representations.

Decoration, then, has its limits as regards the beautiful; it has also its limits as respects the actors. Although, as we have remarked already, they are subservient to the poet, they are, on the other hand, of
primary consequence in relation to the scene. So
much of the costume or the scenery as calls off attention from the actor, is excess; and if an audience be
attracted to 'Lear' or 'Othello' because in the one
drama they will find an exact representation of British
life, and in the other of Venetian magnificence, the
purpose would be better answered by a panorama. In
fact, our present managers seem unwittingly hurry-
ing into an error which both the Athenians and the
Romans committed in such matters centuries ago.
At Athens, no expense, latterly, was thought too

great for the service of the theatre. In the midst of wars, the public treasury was heavily taxed on behalf of the Dionysiac festivals; private fortunes were squandered upon the equipment of the choruses; gold and ivory and silk were lavished upon the proscenium, the altar, and the players' dresses. Yet in the very same age an act was passed forbidding the master-works of the three great Athenian dramatists to be acted, and commanding them to be read at the Bacchic solemnities. Tragedy was buried under its own pomp; money could not supply the dearth of befitting actors; the Athenians had not resolution enough to check scenic excess, though they had taste enough to guard Æschylus and Sophocles from its consequences.

At Rome, where the artistic sensibilities of the people were blunt and coarse, for the most part, decoration, as might be expected, more rapidly surpassed its limits, and the drama degenerated into pantomime. After Roscius and Æsopus quitted the stage, we find no records of either comic or tragic actors of eminence. In less than one generation these excellent artists were succeeded by Bathyllus and Pylades, who, surrounded by crowded *groupes* and dazzling draperies, *danced* the parts of Hercules and Agamemnon to thunders of applause.

In the days when the drama attempted less and succeeded better, elocution was a regular branch of an actor's education. It may be so still; but we

rarely discover traces of the art of speaking being
taught, or at least acquired, to any purpose. Except,
indeed, at the only two theatres where Shakespeare
is still represented, elocution, for any ends to be answered, may as well drop into the rank of *artes deper-
ditæ*. But even at what may be termed our only
classical theatres, we miss the careful modulation
of voice and rhythm which we can remember as
generally prevailing at Covent-Garden under the
Kemble dynasty. To it has succeeded, where any
system at all is followed, an inharmonious mode of
declamation which causes prose to be undistinguish-
able from verse, and even prose itself to forego its
proper cadences and proportions. It is called, we
believe, a more natural manner of speaking. But do
those who term it so weigh well their own designation? When men and women in ordinary life and
upon ordinary topics speak in harmonious numbers,
it will be right for the actor to hold the mirror up to
life, and imitate them. But as men and women do
not, and never will speak in the melodious cadences
of heroic verse, the actor has no right to consider
their common speech as his rule for enunciating the
lofty and passionate thoughts of 'Hamlet' and 'Macbeth.' *His* strain is cast in a loftier mood, and, while
keeping clear from vulgar rant and bombast, should
be resonant of the harmonics with which he is entrusted. It requires, as it has been well said, a
man of genius to introduce and make current a po-

pular fallacy. Mr. Macready was unquestionably a man of genius, and as unquestionably, in our judgment, inoculated his profession with a style of elocution which sets poetry, music, and nature alike at defiance.

We have been oftentimes puzzled to account for the principles upon which this much-admired actor founded his theory and practice of enunciation. For that it was a theory, however erroneous and perverse, must be obvious to all who, like ourselves, remember the earlier and better representations of that gentleman. His voice was then full, free, and undisturbed by affectation; the sentiments or passions to which he gave utterance seemed in those days to spring from genuine emotions of his heart; the rhythm of verse was distinctly marked; the cadence and the meaning of prose were carefully conveyed. Whereas in his latter years he adopted a manner of which the only merit was distinctness of utterance. To grace, to verisimilitude, or to harmony, it made no pretensions; indeed, it seemed carefully to shun these qualities, as so many needless excrescences of declamation. Nor was he content with practising his theory himself; his brother actors were sedulously trained in the same school, and many of them very effectively copied their master. Unfortunately, his disciples are yet extant, and we must await another generation of actors before this heresy of the tongue shall have quite run out its sands.

One of the most disheartening circumstances of the modern drama to all parties really interested in its conservation as a rational entertainment is, the present fashion for parodies of sterling plays. We know not whether the manager, the actor, or the public at large be the greater sufferer by this epidemic nuisance. Of the authors of such monstrosities we cannot write with sufficient contempt : the most successful, and at the same time the most hideous of parodists are monkeys; and we rate no higher the preposterous blockheads who convert into mirth and laughter the solemn and serious scenes of Shakespeare. To a manager who entertains higher notions of his art and position than that of a mere snare or trap-fall for audiences, they are directly injurious; for, on the one hand, they divert from his house the just remuneration of his pains and outlay, and on the other, they operate as temptations to him to forego his efforts in the right path, and to become a mere caterer for one of the vulgarest of tastes, a taste for the low and ludicrous. The right place for managers who so cater for the public is Greenwich Fair. To the actors, again, burlesque is baneful, inasmuch as it accustoms them to regard under a distorted aspect the very highest matters of their art. Above all, it is prejudicial to the public. Let us imagine for a moment the effect of a gallery of caricatures, either in painting or sculpture, or rather the indignation which such an affront to the national judgment would, it is to be hoped, elicit.

Yet what would be justly resented in the case of the other arts, is as unjustly applauded and caressed in scenic representations. An Aristophanic sketch, such as Mr. Planché or Mr. Tom Taylor provide for the Saturnalia of Christmas, is indeed legitimate. It shoots folly as it flies, is a lively comment upon current absurdities, and frequently speaks wholesome truths in the accents of timely jest. But burlesques, of which it is the formal purpose to convert into laughter what was meant to exalt and purify the soul, are offences against public taste and morals equally; and that such offences, instead of being promptly silenced, should be applauded and caressed, and that Shakespeare should be especially selected as the butt of these barren witlings, appears to us one of the most decisive symptoms that the Drama, in our generation, is really on the decline.

Our indignation at these foul excrescences of the present stage has led us aside from the main question, namely, whether the drama be truly, as we are so often assured, in a consumptive condition, and whether its revival on any large and liberal scale be no longer practicable. We have enumerated sundry causes adverse to its general prosperity,—the dispersion of the actors over a wider area; the partially antagonistic influences of literature, in supplying some of the excitement which, at a time when readers were comparatively few, the theatre alone afforded; the rash and often unjust rivalry of managers with each

other; and the decay of the provincial schools that
formerly fed the metropolitan stage. Under the present system, we believe these causes of disadvantage to
be irremediable. But is the present the only practicable system, and is it indeed too late to devise or
apply some efficient remedy? Of the three parties
concerned in the welfare or rehabilitation of the
drama, one—the actor himself—is nearly powerless,
and must be put nearly aside. By his very articles
of agreement, he must do the manager's bidding, and
to do that bidding effectually, as well for his employer
as for his own reputation, he must humour the fancies
of the public. The possible cure of the alleged evils
therefore rests with the managers and their audiences;
and we are of opinion that some terms of accommo-
dation may be discovered for their common and respective advantage.

Numerically considered, we do not think that the
race of play-goers is diminished. This indeed is a subject for statistics. Relatively to certain classes, their
number has undoubtedly declined, since, although we
comfortably plume ourselves upon possessing the most
magnificent dramatic poetry in the world, we rather
inconsistently eschew its representation, and flock
to entertainments imperfectly understood by two-
thirds of the spectators. Does any reasonable being
affect to think that the opera is much more than a
splendid pantomime to at least half its frequenters, or
that Rachel and Devrient are verily and indeed ap-

preciated by all who applaud them and at the same
time invidiously contrast them with English actors?
To answer these questions affirmatively demands faith
bigger than a grain of mustard-seed, and more than,
we confess, we individually own to having. Yet from
the practice of the Opera House and the St. James's
Theatre, we discern some hopes of recovery for our
own. The hours observed by these establishments
are better adapted to the usages of society; the performances are not overloaded by quantity; the actors
are not tasked and jaded beyond their strength. Our
proposal has not indeed novelty to recommend it; the
novelty would consist in a fair trial whether a later
hour for commencing performances, a more strict
adhesion to separate classes of performance at different theatres, and, above all, a shorter period of de-
tention in a heated atmosphere, might not be found
more attractive to the public and more remunerative
to the manager. Three hours of recreation may be
pleasant, or at least may well be endured. By eight
o'clock in the evening dinner might be comfortably
concluded, and even the process of digestion as comfortably commenced. By eleven o'clock both eye and
ear would be satiated with seeing and hearing, and
some appetite left for a future gratification of those
senses. The cost and cares of the manager would be
lessened by twelve hours in each week—no inconsiderable relief, one would think, in the course of a year,
—while the actor, by such curtailment, would also be

less physically wearied, and acquire leisure for a maturer study and elaboration of his characters. As all
previous plans, according to the chroniclers of the
stage, have failed in securing any long course of dramatic prosperity, it would be running no great risk
to make one experiment more—an experiment which,
whatever its demerits or disadvantages, would have at
least this recommendation, that by shortening the
time it would abridge the sufferings of all the parties
concerned.

Dramatic authors, brazened, we suppose, by custom,
make no scruple, nowadays, of avowing their debts
to their French originals, and even seem to take a
certain degree of pride in publishing their importations from the opposite shore. We find no fault with
the practice, provided always that our home-born
authors are really as impotent as they make themselves out to be, since it is better to borrow than to
be quite penniless. This however is a matter on
which they, not we, are the best judges. Meanwhile
habemus confitentes reos, and live in an age of adaptation. We incline to think however that our actors
might in some respects, and with general advantage
to themselves, take a leaf now and then from their
authors' books, and import a few hints from their
foreign brethren. From the French comedians they
might learn that the art of acting is not a mere outline, but a careful filling-up of character ; and from
the Germans they might copy a conscientious car-

nestness in presenting their author's sense in appropriate artistic forms. In these respects, more than
in any actual superiority of gifts, external or internal,
consist, in our opinion, the real advantages of foreign
artists above our own.

We do not however belong to that comfortless race
of beings whose delight is to travel from Dan to
Beersheba, and to cry, "All is barren;" neither would
we invidiously refer to an exotic stage alone for all
that is excellent in dramatic art, and to our own
merely to find fault. Could our performers be more
efficiently concentrated than they are, our managers
be induced to aim at the discipline of their companies
rather than at the novelty or variety of their productions, and the public be led to regard the stage itself
as one among the schools of art, we should not despair of the English Drama becoming once more an
amusement of the more refined classes of society, even
as it was when Ministers of State complimented Booth
from the side-boxes, or the circles at Holland House
assisted at the performances of Kemble and Mrs.
Siddons. We have tendered these imperfect suggestions with an earnest wish that the theatre may one
day be restored to the position it once occupied among
the pleasures of refined and instructed persons, instead
of being, as it now too commonly is, regarded as a
trivial or a dull employment of an evening. The nation which boasts of Shakespeare and his great contemporaries, and which produced the family of the

Kembles, should continue to boast of its stage.   But in order to become a subject of legitimate pride, the stage itself must retrace many a long and heedless step in the path of error, and, by assuming to itself a vocation to guide rather than follow the caprices of the public, regain the grounds at least of self-respect, before it can re-acquire its true position among the arts which minister to the instruction as well as to the amusement of an age.

SONGS FROM THE DRAMATISTS.*

———◆———

THE popularization of literature has been accompanied by evil results as well as good. The number of readers has infinitely increased, but the quality of literature has almost in equal measure been deteriorated. With a few honourable and striking exceptions, few recent authors exhibit any masculine strength or idiomatic raciness of language; as few books display any depth of learning or originality of thought. The people like easy reading, and there is a superfœtation of it. We have abundance of pungent sauces, but little strong meat to eat with them. We have a plenteous crop of literary gossip, but the garners in which our elder and manlier literature is stored are seldom opened. Our great writers are talked about, not read.

Probably this partial oblivion of the classics of our language will outlast the present generation. Popular

---

* Reprinted from 'Fraser's Magazine,' November, 1854.

Songs from the Dramatists. Edited by Robert Bell. *Annotated Edition of the English Poets.* London: John W. Parker and Son, 1854.

literature must be drunk down to the very lees before
it will awaken any real weariness of the flesh in its
readers.   The excess of the evil will work its own
cure; and when the age has been sated with books
that demand no more attention than is consistent
with the whirl of a railway or the leisure of a club,
our descendants may revert to the substantial diet of
their and our ancestors.   We do not despair of a revival of a taste for Bolingbroke's prose or Spenser's
verse; although the date of that revival may be as
remote as the glimpse of power and glory which the
son of Beor caught from the hills of Moab.   The
fulfilment of the vision was neither soon nor near,
but it came in the end.

With these anticipations, we greet with no ordinary
pleasure the republication of some of our established
poets in a form accessible to the many, and yet sufficiently critical for the few.   Of cheap and hasty
reprints we have more than enough — editions so
slovenly and inaccurate that they would disgrace a
Californian journeyman working against time, illustrated by notes which add to the previous ignorance
of the reader the ignorance and blunders of the editor
also.   In such hands, Gibbon becomes inexact, and
Cowper breaks Priscian's head.   Such taskwork would
be as harmless as it is disreputable, were it not that
an ill-edited book goes down with the "patient public," and obstructs and discourages honest underta-
kings of a similar kind.   We have sometimes been

at the pains to draw up a list of editorial or typo-graphical blunders in single volumes of a popular series, and we may one day produce it for the benefit of the unwary. But we have now a more agreeable purpose in view,—that, namely, of directing the at-tention of our readers to an edition of the English poets which forms a remarkable contrast to the "Brummagem ware" so commonly hawked about as a genuine article.

The 'Annotated Edition of the English Poets,' under the careful supervision of Mr. Robert Bell, has now reached its tenth volume. We employ the word "care-ful" advisedly. Dr. Dibdin, indeed, occasionally spoke of "immaculate editions" — a phrase which proved that the learned doctor was one of that class of readers whom Jeremy Taylor deprecates as "men who read after supper." We make no such pretensions on Mr. Bell's behalf, but we maintain that he well merits the designation of a *careful* editor. For, in the first place, he has, on every occasion, reverted to the most reliable and authentic text of his authors—whether it be found in an early or a late edition. He has expunged the errors and amended the caprices of former editions; he has rescued many a passage from the repeated blunders of printers, and—no trifling service to all parties, the dead as well as the living—has heedfully adopted a consistent scheme of punctuation. "Of our pleasant vices the Gods make whips to scourge us," and this is just measure; but it is not meting

justly, to twist a rod out of our merits, and apply it
to our backs. Yet this is the measure which, from
some quarters, has been dealt, heaped and running
over, to the editor of this series of English Poets.
Mr. Bell's care in punctuation has been alleged as a
proof of carelessness — the real culprits being the
editors or printers who left the work of correction to
be done now at this the eleventh hour. The readings
which he has deliberately preferred have been adduced
as examples of his incompetency; the fact being all
the while that he has in most instances restored to
his authors the meaning and the phrase which they
originally wrote. It would be hardly worth while
noticing the perverse judgments passed upon his
critical labours, were it not that the public will not
sift these points for itself, and thinks—*regis ad ex-
emplar*—just as some puny whipster with his pen
pleases to dictate. Let any one with sound sense, a
competent acquaintance with the revolutions in our
language, a tolerable knowledge of early editions, and
above all, without a previous intention to find or make
faults, examine Mr. Bell's text of Wyatt, Oldham,
Dryden, and Cowper, beside the most authentic texts
of those authors, and we will ensure a verdict in his
favour, whether it be accompanied or not with a censure of the adverse counsel and witnesses. In taking
his stand upon an approved although not always the
adopted text of the poets hitherto edited by him, Mr.
Bell has judiciously availed himself of the practice of

the late Robert Southey. Does the reader happen to
be aware that the version of Cowper's 'Homer' which
Southey adopted in his edition of the poet's works, is
the translation which he made at Olney, and not the
translation which he revised at Dunham Lodge; the
version which he produced when comparatively sane
in mind and sound in body, and not the version
which he retouched and enfeebled after his eye had
grown dim and his malady had permanently established itself? Again, in Southey's edition of the
'Pilgrim's Progress' we have the *ipsissima verba* of
Bunyan's vision, cleared from the errors of generations of printers, and from the interpolations of generations of editors. We have even more than this;
for in reading the text of Bunyan's own first edition,
we read the words of the Dream as they welled fresh
from his imagination. Bunyan himself, in his own
later impressions of his work, occasionally used the
hoe too rashly, and extirpated more than once or
twice the flowers with the weeds. The wise in such
matters are now pretty unanimous in thinking that
both Cowper and Bunyan are under considerable post-
humous obligations to Dr. Southey; and if they have
since met in any habitable planet, both the rhyming
and the unrhyming poet may have tendered him their
acknowledgments for the same. We trust that similar justice will be rendered to Mr. Bell, not indeed in
Elysium, but by the present generation. We do not
grudge him any post-obit applause, but we trust that

his merits will be recognized while he is yet able to respond to a vote of thanks.

We gladly turn away from the ungracious task of noticing absurd and groundless depreciation. The pleasanter office now awaits us of briefly surveying the contents of one of the best conceived and most agreeable volumes of the present series of English Poets. The 'Songs from the Dramatists' is a collection that would have cheered the soul of Charles Lamb, and may stand beside his delightful 'Specimens of the Dramatic Poets.' It is a book which, had it existed fifty years ago, might have spared Dr. Aikin the trouble of writing his foolish essay on song-writing; a book that would have drawn from Hazlitt some genial criticism and many sparkling periods; a book that would have found its place in the library at Abbotsford beside the 'Border Minstrelsy,' and been carried by Shelley in his rambles through the pine-forest of Ravenna; a book for a rainy day, for a summer noon, for an evening at yule-tide, for intervals of business, for any time and season. Perhaps the title hardly expresses the full import of this little volume's contents. The term Song, as commonly accepted, is not sufficiently indicative of its lyrical wealth. The incantation scene from 'Macbeth,' the solemn dirges of our old playwrights, the lyric portions of the 'Faithful Shepherdess,' can scarcely be included in that category. It is seldom that a title-page professes too little; and Mr. Bell's is certainly

not among those censured by Democritus Junior, as
"Conceited in its inscription, and able (as Pliny
quotes out of Seneca) to make him loyter by the way
that went in haste to fetch a midwife for his daughter." Neither is it such a frontispiece as Milton
deemed attractive to "the stall-reader." We are not
prepared on the instant with a better prefix, and
"good wine needs no bush." Yet perhaps it were
more germane to the matter to have entitled the
book, ' Songs, Grave and Gay, from the Dramatists.'

Why has Milton been denied his rightful privilege
of contributing his *symbolon* to this feast of lyrical
delicacies? The editor has most properly culled
more than one garland from Ben Jonson's Masques,
and from a poem from which Milton did not disdain
to borrow—Fletcher's 'Faithful Shepherdess.' " *Cur
à convivantibus exulat philosophia ?*"—wherefore does
not the name of ' Comus ' appear in the table of contents? It cannot have been negligence in the editor.
'Comus' was not indeed like Jonson's Masques, "presented at Court," yet it was enacted at Ludlow Castle.
Surely in a second edition this defect will be amended,
and Milton's Masque be allowed the privilege of *post-
liminium.*

The ' Songs from the Dramatists,' like the dramas
in which they are imbedded, may be properly divided
into three periods : 1, Those which preceded Shakespeare ; 2, The songs of Shakespeare, and, *longo in-
tervallo,* those of his immediate contemporaries ; and

3, Those which were produced after the great dramatic era had closed. The lyrical productions of the first of these periods exhibit, like its drama, a spasmodic strength and an irregular sweetness, "native wood-notes wild," springing frequent out of the bosom of dissonance. The language, indeed, was in too transitional a condition to admit of the perfect elaboration which song-writing demands. Potent masters in the art of rhyme as were Chaucer and Spenser, and skilful and sweet as Surrey and Wyatt approved themselves to be, the chords they struck, if not always of a higher mood than song requires, were too generally elaborate and full for the seeming spontaneity of feeling that most aptly weds itself to music. These early songs savour of village mirth, of the pipe and tabor, and the accompaniment of rustical feet. Their music does not float upon the air; their gushes of sweet sound do not imprison the senses; they do not cling to our memories; they could not be sung by tricksy spirits, hardly by very tuneful mortals: in portions beautiful exceedingly, as wholes they are seldom pleasing. The most finished of them—such as " Cupid and Campaspe played "—savour rather of Bion and Moschus and the Greek Anthology, than of sterling English melody. Fully assenting to Mr. Bell's admiration of this song of Lyly the Euphuist, we prefer for its easy measure and joyous cadence the duet (if we may venture on so modern a phrase) between Paris and Ænone, in Peele's ' Arraignment of Paris.'

" *Æn.*   Fair and fair, and twice so fair,
          As fair as any may be;
          The fairest shepherd on our green,
          A love for any lady.
Par.   Fair and fair, and twice so fair,
          As fair as any may be:
          Thy love is fair for thee alone,   .
          And for no other lady.
Æn.   My love is fair, my love is gay,
          As fresh as bin the flowers in May,
          And of my love my roundelay,
          My merry, merry, merry roundelay,
          Concludes with Cupid's curse,
          They that do change old love for new,
          Pray gods, they change for worse!
Ambo, simul. They that do change, etc.
Æn.   Fair and fair, etc.
Par.   Fair and fair, etc.   .
Æn.   My love can pipe, my love can sing,
          My love can many a pretty thing,
          And of his lovely praises ring
          My merry, merry roundelays,
          Amen to Cupid's curse,
          They that do change, etc."

That the poets of this period included in the term
"song" poems which can hardly have been accompanied by music, appears from the following verses
of the same author.   It would tax the art of Sir
Henry Bishop himself to adapt them to either wind
or stringed instrument.   Probably their only accompaniment was an occasional note of the rebeck or
cittern.

"THE AGED MAN-AT-ARMS.

" His golden locks time hath to silver turned;
          O time too swift, O swiftness never ceasing!

F

His youth 'gainst time and age hath ever spurned,
  But spurned in vain ; youth waneth by encreasing.
Beauty, strength, youth, are flowers but fading seen :
Duty, faith, love, are roots, and ever green.

" His helmet now shall make a hive for bees,
  And lovers' songs be turned to holy psalms ;
A man-at-arms must now serve on his knees,
  And feed on prayers, which are old age's alms :
But though from court to cottage he depart,
His saint is sure of his unspotted heart.

" And when he saddest sits in homely cell,
  He'll teach his swains this carol for a song :
' Blessed be the hearts that wish my Sovereign well,
  Cursed be the souls that think her any wrong.'
Goddess, allow this aged man his right,
To be your beadsman now that was your knight."

The song-writers of this period were deeply imbued
with at least the images and allusions derived from
the Roman Poets.   Apollo and Syrinx, Daphne and
Pan, Cupid and Endymion are used by them as fami-
liarly as by those intolerably tedious personages, the
composers of pastorals and madrigals for the Court of
Versailles.   In the time of Peele, Heywood, and Lyly,
these mythological beings were not, however, merely
vapid abstractions, the counterparts of the be-wigged
lords and be-painted ladies who delighted in making
or pretending to make love after the manner of the
ancients.   In the sixteenth century literature retained
its freshness ; the most excellent books were written
in the language of ancient Greece or Rome ; the
mirrors and the models of lyrical composition were

imported from semi-pagan Italy. Tedious as they now appear to us, these graceful incarnations of heathen sentiment were suggestive and impressive to our forefathers.

The simple dramatic agencies available and employed in our elder theatre, imposed upon the song-writer of the time heavier duties than those which devolve upon his modern representative. The inanities of a song were not then concealed by the crash of an orchestra: the pipe, viol, and theorbo left the poet's words audible; an indifferent ballad was not rescued from the pit by the charms or the skill of popular bass or sopranos. A song was often a very serious matter, recommending itself to the general ear and heart by pregnant saws and ethical maxims. Samuel Daniel's poem—we can scarcely imagine it set to music—entitled 'The Influence of Opinion,' reads like a passage from Seneca "done into metre;" nor was Daniel more gloomy and sententious than the satirical and acrimonious Nash, meditating "on graves, and worms, and epitaphs," in the following lines, entitled—

"APPROACHING DEATH.

"Adieu; farewell earth's bliss,
    This world uncertain is:
    Fond are life's lustful joys,
    Death proves them all but toys.
    None from his darts can fly:
    I am sick, I must die.
            Lord have mercy on us!

F 2

· "Rich men, trust not in wealth ;
 Gold cannot buy you health ;
 Physic himself must fade ;
 All things to end are made ;
 The plague full swift goes by ;
 I am sick, I must die.
     Lord have mercy on us !

"Beauty is but a flower,
 Which wrinkles will devour :
 Brightness falls from the air ;
 Queens have died young and fair ;
 Dust hath closed Helen's eye ;
 I am sick, I must die.
     Lord have mercy on us !

"Strength stoops unto the grave :
 Worms feed on Hector brave.
 Swords may not fight with fate :
 Earth still holds ope her gate.
 Come, come, the bells do cry ;
 I am sick, I must die.
     Lord have mercy on us !

"Wit with his wantonness,
 Tasteth death's bitterness.
 Hell's executioner
 Hath no ears for to hear
 What vain art can reply ;
 I am sick, I must die.
     Lord have mercy on us !

"Haste therefore each degree
 To welcome destiny :
 Heaven is our heritage,
 Earth but a player's stage.
 Mount we unto the sky ;
 I am sick, I must die.
     Lord have mercy on us !"

We have dwelt the longer upon these earlier samples of English song-writing, partly because they show the latitude which our ancestors accorded to this species of composition, and partly because they exhibit the full Pallas-like completeness with which the art of song-writing sprang from the imagination, or rather from the heart, of Shakespeare. But before we enter upon the second and most brilliant period of the lyrical accompaniment of the English drama, we must take a rapid glance at some of Mr. Bell's biographical notices of the poets themselves. The employments and conditions of the authors will furnish us with some clue to the quality and character of their productions.

When Macklin was asked why he forsook the stage, for which he had some genius, and took up lecturing on history and science, for which he assuredly had none, he replied that the latter was the more gentlemanly occupation. It would seem that writing of songs was accounted of yore a gentlemanly occupation also. For although the majority of writers who have been laid under contribution by Mr. Bell were playwrights proper, yet we find among them a fair sprinkling of poets who had other means of putting money in their purses. The very first name that leads off the dance is that of Nicholas Udall, who, descended from Peter Lord Uvedale and Nicholas Udall, Constable of Winchester Castle in the reign of Edward III., was himself head-master of Eton, and previously a scholar in high repute of Corpus Christi College,

Oxford. Nicholas, however, was more clever than
clean-handed. At Eton he was the *plagosus Orbilius*
of the sixth form; and dismissed from his master-
ship for stealing spoons. He seems, indeed, to have
regained his character, since he died head-master of
Westminster College, besides holding a fair share of
Church preferment,—"a stall at Windsor, and the
living of Calborne, in the Isle of Wight." Nicholas
owed something to his gifts as a dramatic writer, and
his skill in composing dialogues and interludes to be
performed at Court. Yet these talents alone would
hardly have helped him out of the spoon scrape, had
he not been a shrewd controversialist on the winning
side. His advocacy of the doctrines of Protestantism
in King Edward's reign, cast a veil over his delin-
quencies. How he escaped scorching in Queen Mary's
reign we are not told.

In John Still we have another instance of clerical
melody. Of his history, says Mr. Bell, "little is
known beyond the incidents of his preferments in the
Church." And he seems to have merited advance-
ment; for Sir John Harrington, Queen Elizabeth's
godson, speaks of him as of a man to whom he never
came but he grew more religious, and from whom he
never went but he parted more instructed. We
have not room for the list of his preferments; be it
remembered, however, that he died Bishop of Bath
and Wells, and wrote one of the most genial incen-
tives to deep potations in the language,—

    "Back and side go bare, go bare;"

even now chanted on fitting occasions at Cambridge supper-parties. Again in Dr. Jasper Mayne we have an example of the diversity of gifts, if not of the same spirit; for he was at once a distinguished preacher and a dramatic author. From the sample of his wit as it appears in his comedy of 'The City Match,' we are not indeed inclined to estimate it highly. Yet of his being a practical humorist there can be no doubt, if the following anecdote of him be true. The Doctor had an old servant, to whom he bequeathed a trunk, which he told him contained something that would make him drink after his death. When, on the Doctor's demise, the box was opened, it was found to contain a red-herring! This is a livelier jest than any to be found in his comedy; but perhaps he reserved a richer vein of humour for the pulpit, and punned and quibbled like the facetious Dr. South. In looking over Mr. Bell's biographical introductions to his 'Book of Songs,' we have been much struck with the liberal quota of authors supplied to the theatre by our Universities, and by Cambridge especially. As yet the study of the severer sciences had not frozen the genial current of the lyric Muse. We suspect, however, that although Heywood, Peele, Nash, and others were dignified with the addition of M.A. to their names, they were such scions as the University not unwillingly saw grafted upon other stocks, and that *Alma Mater* rejoiced when these her *fast* sons betook themselves to the more congenial sphere of a

London playhouse. It is indeed curious to contrast
the roving and extravagant lives of these jovial blades
with the picture of college life drawn by old Latimer,
who preceded them by one generation only. It is
difficult to conceive that the shivering and half-
starved scholars who ran up and down the cloisters
to warm themselves, and supped on thin mutton-broth,
can ever have burgeoned forth into writers of mirthful roundelays.

We are almost inclined to pass over the 'Songs of
Shakespeare' with a simple reference to their absolute royalty of perfection, both *à parte ante* and *à
parte post*,—both as regards all compositions of this
order which preceded them, and all which followed
them. It is superfluous to commend the violet for its
perfume, the sweet South for the odours it breathes,
the lilies of the field for their purity, or the voice of
the nightingale for its sweetness. They are as much
better than the songs of Burns, as the songs of Burns
are better than those of Moore. The secret of their
structure is beyond alchemy. We can divide a ray
of light, and dive to the fountains of colour, and trace
the flower from its seed, and map the stars, and re-
duce the diamond to its elements, and apply the laws
of harmony to the songs of birds. But we do not
know the secret of Shakespeare's supremacy in song-
writing,—

"Nil majus generatur ipso,
Nec viget quidquam simile aut secundum."

Shelley was wont to say that the poetry of Dante filled him with despair : and beside Shakespeare's songs all others appear to disadvantage. " The words of Mercury are harsh after the songs of Apollo." In this kind of writing, as in every other, Shakespeare had an instinctive knowledge of the " great arcanum." His was at once " the art that adds to nature " and " the art that nature makes." With other song-writers some proper and personal characteristic may be discerned ; the individuality peeps through the sentiments or the words; it is the outward and visible sign of the inward and spiritual life of the writer. In Beaumont and Fletcher we find variety, grace, and sweetness ; in Jonson, a sturdy purpose and a learned taste, wringing, as it were, beauty and melody from book-lore; in Middleton, a luxuriant fancy ; in Webster, uncontrolled passion and earnest eloquence. In Shakespeare alone we meet with all these qualities combined—passion and tenderness, gaiety and grace, the subtlest wit, the most natural wood-notes, the most rare combinations, and full-throated ease. Nor is the variety of his songs less admirable than their excellence, or their dramatic propriety less wonderful than their variety. He has married to music the grief and the joy, the aspirations and the circum-stances of all sorts and conditions of men. In them find fitting utterance the lover, the student, the clown, the courtier, the high-born beauty, the country mal-kin, the warrior arming for the fight, the grave-digger making the house that lasts till doomsday, royalty on its funeral couch, the tricksy spirits of the air, the train of the faery king, the foul earthworm Caliban, the ancient gods of Olympus, the chant of wizards, and the dirge of death.

The step from Shakespeare to his contemporaries, great and manifold as were their poetical excellencies, is like the passage of Christian from the Delectable Mountains to the lower valley, with its bright ver- dure, its narrow causeway, and its frequent pit-falls. We have stepped from the Eden of song into a lower region, often " beautiful exceedingly," yet not un- vexed by storms nor exempt from change. It is re- markable that Jonson, whose genius, from its general characteristics, appears to have been ill-adapted to the delicate task of song-writing, should yet have produced so many melodious and graceful productions of this order. As in his plays, so in his lyrical effu- sions, Jonson wrought by line and rule. His mind was as richly stored as Milton's with the lore of Greece and Rome. He merited even in a higher de- gree than Beaumont the appellation of "judicious." But he possessed little or no spontaneity. He built up his songs as he constructed his dramas—line upon line, and phrase upon phrase. He was, like Gray, a consummate artist in the mosaic of poetry. Yet it is unjust to accuse Jonson of pedantry. Books were to him a substantial life; he thought through them, he saw with them; they were to him in the place of heart and imagination. But he availed himself of their aid in no servile spirit; and though he borrowed largely, he mostly repaid his loans with liberal interest. In the songs of Jonson, Mr. Bell judiciously remarks:—

"We have great command of resources, and a visible air of preparation. The lines are thoughtful, and occasionally rugged, and must be read, even in the singing, with a certain degree of emphasis and deliberation. They do not spring at once to the heart and fancy. The spirit of the Greek Anthology is in them, and is felt either in the allusions, the phrase, the subject, or the diction. If they do not recall the ravishing music of the lark or the nightingale, they hold us in the spell of some fine instrument whose rich notes are delivered with the skill of a master."

Jonson's masques, songs, and pastoral scenes have suffered from unmerited neglect. It has been too hastily assumed that his *forte* lay in the delineation of humorous or, more properly, of eccentric character. But "out of the eater came forth meat, and out of the strong, sweetness;" and "rare Ben Jonson" occasionally relaxed his iron sinews, and welded on his anvil a network of verse as fine and enthralling as the web in which Hephaistos caught Aphrodite and Ares. We take for granted that his songs 'Come, my Celia, let us prove,' and 'Still to be neat, still to be drest,' are familiar to the reader. The two following have less frequently found their way into extracts from the

English poets.   This reads like a fragment of Stesi-
chorus imbedded in one of Plato's dialogues.

> "So beauty on the waters stood,
>   When love had severed earth from flood;
>   So when he parted air from fire,
>   He did with concord all inspire;
>   And there a matter he then taught
>   That elder than himself was thought;
>   Which thought was yet the child of earth,
>   For Love is older than his birth."

'Echo mourning the death of Narcissus,' is conceived in the spirit of the tender and melancholy
Simonides.

> "Slow, slow, fresh fount, keep time with my salt tears;
>   Yet slower, yet, O faintly gentle springs:
> List to the heavy part the music bears,
>   Woe weeps out her division when she sings.
>   Droop, herbs and flowers;   .
>   Fall, grief, in showers;
>   Our beauties are not ours;
>   Oh, I could still,
> Like melting snow upon some craggy hill,
>   Drop, drop, drop, drop,
> Since nature's pride is, now, a withered daffodil."

In the following song, entitled 'Love and Death,'
which occurs in his fine dramatic pastoral 'The Sad
Shepherd,'—a poem of which Mr. Bell remarks, that
"it abounds in passages of exquisite beauty, and displays his mastery over a species of poetry in which
he is least appreciated,"—the learned allusions are
singularly at variance with the condition of the song-
stress, yet there is a grace even in its discrepancy:—

"Though I am young and cannot tell
　　Either what death or love is, well,
　Yet I have heard they both bear darts,
　And both do aim at human hearts;
　And then again, I have been told,
　Love wounds with heat, as death with cold;
　So that I fear they do but bring
　Extremes to touch, and mean one thing.

" As in a ruin we it call,
　　One thing to be blown up, or fall;
　Or to our end, like way may have,
　By a flash of lightning or a wave:
　So love's inflamèd shaft or brand,
　May kill as soon as death's cold hand;
　Except love's fires the virtue have
　To fright the frost out of the grave."

Beaumont and Fletcher's songs "occupy a middle
region between Shakespeare's and Jonson's." Whatever "Beaumont's judgment" may have been, we are
inclined to ascribe to his copartner in dramatic composition the principal share in the writing of their
songs. Fletcher's ear for metrical melody was of
the finest order, and the music of his verse has often
recommended his dramas to the closet, when they
have been feeble and ineffectual on the stage. We do
not, indeed, pretend to trace in their joint productions the marks of either individual hand. We have
not much respect for the tradition—and it is nothing
more than tradition—that Beaumont contributed the
controlling judgment, and Fletcher the abundant
fancy and the exuberant wit. But Fletcher, although
the elder of the twain, survived Beaumont many

years, and is the undoubted author of many plays
over which his associate exercised no superintendence;
and in these very plays occur for the most part the
most finished and delicate proofs of the lyrical genius
of the surviving poet.   There is also in Fletcher's
songs a genial and hearty element of mirth, which
makes us regret that in his dramas he should so often
have curbed his humorous vein, and preferred brilliant but hard scintillations of wit.   In this latter
respect, indeed, Fletcher was the dramatical parent of
Congreve, and introduced the evil habit of putting
into the mouth of his clowns, repartees only proper
to his "curled darlings" and courtiers.   "Tell me if
Congreve's fools *be* fools indeed," is a censure equally
applicable to the comic personages of Fletcher.   His
rustics are fine gentlemen in smock-frocks; his beggars might graduate in the Academy of Compliments,
and walk gowned with "Biron, Longueville, and Du-
main."

Of Fletcher's power for representing genial mirth,
the following song from the 'Spanish Curate' affords
a proof; as the drama itself from which the song is
taken evinces that Fletcher went astray in preferring
sparkling wit to the natural humour which he kept
under restraint.

> " Let the bells ring, and let the boys sing,
>   The young lasses skip and play ;
> Let the cups go round, till round goes the ground ;
>   Our learnèd old vicar will stay.

" Let the pig turn merrily, merrily, ah !
 And let the fat goose swim ;
For verily, verily, verily, ah !
 Our vicar this day shall be trim.

" The stewed cock shall crow, cock-a-loodle-loo,
 A loud cock-a-loodle shall he crow ;
The duck and the drake shall swim in a lake
 Of onions and claret below.

" Our wives shall be neat, to bring in our meat
 To thee our most noble adviser ;
Our pains shall be great, and bottles shall sweat,
 And we ourselves will be wiser.

" We 'll labour and swink, we 'll kiss and we 'll drink,
 And tithes shall come thicker and thicker ;
We 'll fall to our plough, and get children enow,
 And thou shalt be learnèd old vicar."

This roundelay exhibits a singular contrast to the
quaint and tender fancy of a love-song from the same
drama.

" Dearest, do not delay me,
 Since, thou knowest, I must be gone ;
Wind and tide, 't is thought, doth stay me,
 But 't is wind that must be blown
  From that breath whose native smell
  Indian odours far excel.

" Oh, then speak, thou fairest fair !
 Kill not him that vows to serve thee ;
But perfume this neighbouring air,
 Else dull silence, sure, will starve me :
  'T is a word that 's quickly spoken,
  Which, being restrained, a heart is broken."

We pass over Aspasia's song in the 'Maid's Tragedy,' since that play is among the best-known, al-

though by no means, in our judgment, among the happier efforts of Fletcher's muse : the following song from the 'Elder Brother' may be less familiar, and its gracefulness at least atone for its repetition.

> " Beauty clear and fair,
>   · Where the air
>   Rather like a perfume dwells ;
>   Where the violet and the rose
>   Their blue veins in blush disclose,
>   And seem to honour nothing else
>
> " Where to live near,
>   And planted there,
>   Is to live, and still live new ;
>   Where to gain a favour is
>   More than light, perpetual bliss,—
>   Make me live by serving you.
>
> " Dear, again back recall
>   To this light,
>   A stranger to himself and all ;
>   Both the wonder and the story
>   Shall be yours, and eke the glory ;
>   I am your servant, and your thrall."

With one more extract from Fletcher's 'Beggar's Bush'—a comedy which justly commanded a high panegyric from Coleridge—we must pass on to some of the other song-writers of the seventeenth century. The jollity of beggars in the olden time may, like the epithet "merrie" applied to England generally, be a coinage of the brain ; but assuredly our dramatists seem to have thought that your beggars' weeds were the only wear, and that there was no life like the life on the hillside. Nor does this fancy argue altogether a truant disposition; for the poets of those days were mostly a dependent race, and climbed the stairs and ate the bitter bread of great men's houses. Fletcher, from his dwelling on the Bankside; Jonson, from his chambers "in the alley;" Massinger, humiliated, obscure, and poor, may well have sighed for the freedom from solicitation and ceremony enjoyed by the dwellers in barns and gipsy-tents.

> " Cast our caps and cares away :
> This is beggars' holiday!
> At the crowning of our king,
> Thus we ever dance and sing.
> In the world look out and see,
> Where 's so happy a prince as he ?
> Where the nation lives so free,
> And so merry as do we ?
> Be it peace, or be it war,
> Here at liberty we are,
> And enjoy our ease and rest :
> To the field we are not pressed ;
> Nor are called into the town,
> To be troubled with the gown.
> Hang all offices, we cry,
> And the magistrate too, by !
> When the subsidy's increased,
> We are not a penny sessed ;
> Nor will any go to law
> With the beggar for a straw.
> All which happiness, he brags,
> He doth owe unto his rags."

We have given a very imperfect specimen of the lyrical productions of our great dramatic age; but sufficient samples will have been afforded, if we have

induced our readers to turn to the originals in Mr.
Bell's volume. The era of the Restoration was nearly
as unfavourable to the art of song-writing as it was to
the drama generally. When Comus and his crew
were both the minstrels and the audience, a decline,
if not indeed utter corruption, was inevitable in a
species of composition which, to be noble or winning,
must shun the borders and the region of sensuous
and sinful fantasy. The better songs, indeed, of the
age of Charles II. are not to be found in the play-
books. The Dorsets, Buckhursts, and Sucklings,
wrote amorous ditties of some merit, and naval songs
that were still better. But, as regards the drama,
love and noble sentiments disappear with the reopen-
ing of the theatres, and sensuality takes their place.
In order to render the 'Tempest' palatable to an
audience, Dryden inserted into its ethereal visions a
sexual underplot; and made lawless love, in place of
stirring adventure and Roman stateliness and chivalry, the prominent characteristic of 'Antony and
Cleopatra.' The pure lyrical Muse, when not bol-
stered up by the pomp and obscurity of Cowley, was,
like the Lady in 'Comus,' environed by a bestial herd,
and imprisoned in a magic chair. Voluptuous, and
without taste or sentiment, the songs of that scandalous period reflect the garish daylight of town-life;
they echo the sentiments of Whitehall, and record
the intrigues of the Broad Walk in the Mall. The
Strephons and Chloes assumed the garb of Arcadia,

and employed the language of the bagnio in their Amœbean dialogues. The worst portions of Theocritus, Virgil, and the Italian pastorals were selected as the types of rural innocence; and the grossness of these ideal pictures was enhanced by the liberal adoption of the diction and manners of the masques of Versailles. "Music and sweet poetry agree;" and by a fitting retribution, music, wedded to the lays of the Courtalls and Loveits, degenerated with the poetry which it accompanied. Even Dryden "wrote with his left hand" when he attempted the composition of song, masque, or pastoral.

The transition from the unfettered grace of the earlier songs to the more regular measures of later days, is, we think, first observable in Dryden. The following stanzas, if we except a certain halting of the rhythm, might have been produced a century later :—

> " From the low palace of old father Ocean,
>   Come we in pity our cares to deplore;
>   Sea-racing dolphins are trained for our motion,
>   Moony tides swelling to roll us ashore.
>
> " Every nymph of the flood, her tresses rending,
>   Throws off her armlet of pearl in the main ;
>   Neptune in anguish his charge unattending,
>   Vessels are foundering, and vows are in vain."

And the song of Diana might be sung after a " Darlington meet."

> " With horns and with hounds, I waken the day,
>   And hie to the woodland-walks away;

I tuck up my robe, and am buskined soon,
And tie to my forehead a waxing moon.
I course the fleet stag, unkennel the fox,
And chase the wild goats o'er summits of rocks ;
With shouting and hooting we pierce through the sky,
And Echo turns hunter, and doubles the cry."

Congreve's songs, as might be expected from the
wit of his plays, are witty and epigrammatic : but,
like his plays, they are infected with the coarseness
of feelings and the shallowness of principle which prevailed with more or less intensity so long as the literature of the Restoration retained its hold on the national mind. Indeed, our lyrical and dramatical poets
cannot be said to have entirely escaped from the evil
influences of the Stuart Court earlier than the middle
of the last century. The lash of Pope and the fine
irony of Addison were not implements keen enough
to extirpate the disease. It lingered on the stage and
contaminated song-writing as late as the time of
Cumberland and the younger Colman.

Richard Brinsley Sheridan, with whom the series
of dramatic songsters closes, was, acccording to Mi-
chael Kelly, one of those men who, though unable to
sing two bars of any tune correctly, have yet music
in their souls. He would, in rude fashion, with many
exorbitancies of tone and time, give composers of
music a conception of effects to be produced by voice
or instrument, which they adopted and thanked him
for. He brings up the rear-guard on the present
occasion with great force and spirit, and revives atten-

tion just as it had begun to flag beneath the somewhat soporific madrigals of D'Urfey, Congreve, and
Farquhar. The songs in his opera of the 'Duenna' are
as superior to the productions of the century before,
as they are inferior to those of the Elizabethan age.
They have the sharpness and the grace of a fine in-
taglio: Ovid might have been proud of them: they
have as much tenderness as the best portions of his
'Amores,' and the *tour de malice* of his epigrammatic
couplets. If Sheridan had turned his attention to the
writing of lyrical dramas, Gay would have had a formidable rival for his ' Beggar's Opera.'

In some genial moment, when not too full of the
grape, and not more than usually vexed by duns and
bailiffs, our incomparable Brinsley penned his famous
song, beginning,—

"Oh, the days when I was young,"

not perhaps without some compunction for his own
grizzled hairs and declining powers of enjoyment. It
professes a comfortable philosophy, although not of
the more rigid school. If glees be sung in Hades,
we can fancy Anacreon, Propertius, and Walter de
Mapes joining in the chorus.

We cannot dismiss this excellent collection of
' Songs from the Dramatists' with a merely critical
farewell. Its contents are suggestive of higher and
better thoughts than go to the summation of merits
or demerits. We would look beyond the words and
measures to the writers of these songs and dirges—

these slight yet expressive records of many generations of passion and gaiety, sentiment and fancy, tender and imaginative outpourings of many moods and
minds. A book is no dead congeries of paper and ink
and pasteboard : it is a casket rather of the quintes-
sential and spiritual life of men and generations. It
tells more impressively than storied urn or measured
epitaph, of the griefs which have been borne, the joys
that have been shared, the hopes that have been cherished, the dreams that have been trusted by the myriads whose numbers surpass those of the living. For
these songs are doubly representative, first of their
individual authors, and secondly of the generations in
which they lived. So thought the men of yore, so
felt, so rejoiced they in their allotted span of tribula-
tion and gladness, of youthful love, of sobered anticipations. How many weary and watchful hours, how
many genial and jubilant moments are reflected from
the pages of this little book ! Herein, to all who have
ears to hear, are echoes of the woodland and the solitary chamber, of the hubbub of the market, of the
lonely shore, of the song springing from the heart of
the young, of the pensiveness that grows with the
shadow of years past their noon.

As we turn over these pages, we pass from expressions of mere sensuous enjoyment, from the mirth
wherein there is melancholy, from the vanity of youth
and the delirium of pleasure, from the unsubstantial
delights of wine, and music, and flowers, to the

thoughts which dally with death and the worm;
from the pomp and revelry of the banquet-hall, to the
mould and votive chaplets of the grave; "from ceiled
roofs, to arched coffins;" from that "Old England"
which lay within the limits of the four seas, to this
present England, which spreads its arms eastward and
westward, and sends forth its sons as rulers of the
most ancient of kingdoms, or as conquerors of the
unreclaimed waste. The thoughts and the music of
these songs are a common inheritance to him that
from a crest of the Himalaya surveys the fountains of
the Ganges, and to him that from the Canadian hills
looks northward to the palace of eternal winter.
Therefore would we send forth this little volume with
the benison of "good speed," for it may convey to
regions untrodden by them the brave language of our
fathers; and that language is the bond which, when
England's offsets have parted from the parent stem,
will yet hold together in ties of brotherhood all the
members of that race which, as from a second cradle
in the Caucasus, has wandered from Albion to homes
deep-set in torrid or arctic zones.

THE DRAMA.*

————◆————

WE have no sympathies with persons who regard
with indifference the state and prospects of the drama
as a national amusement. We cannot shut our eyes
to the fact that the noblest dramatic poetry has been
produced at the most brilliant epochs of national
history. We cannot regard with apathy or aversion
a branch of art which delineates and appeals directly
to some of the most earnest and ennobling impulses
of humanity; which, in its graver forms, is auxiliary
to moral refinement, and in its lighter, a healthy im-
plement of satire or of mirth. We do not find that
the nations which have been devoid of theatrical representations have surpassed, either in dignity of
thought or decorum of manners, the far greater number which have cherished and developed a national
stage; on the contrary, we are disposed to consider
these exceptional races—and the exceptions are singularly few—as deficient in the higher arts also, and

* Reprinted from the ' Quarterly Review,' June 1854.
Dramatic Register for 1853.   12mo.

wanting some of the nobler elements of civilization. Admitting the transitory nature of histrionic powers, and their consequent inferiority to the genius which impresses the canvas and the stone with enduring grace and life, we cannot but remember that the names of Roscius and Æsopus are as immortal as those of Cicero and Cæsar; and that the fame of Garrick and Siddons is scarcely less a possession for ever than the conversation of Johnson, the portraits of Reynolds, and the eloquence of Burke. That the stage has too often been applied to unworthy purposes, and reflects too often the coarser features of an era, we allow; but the fault rests as much with the age as with the theatre. The theatre, depending more than any other department of art upon public opinion, complies with rather than thwarts its caprices; and public opinion and the press have it at all times in their power to correct the errors of the stage. Yet it would be unjust to the theatre to deny that it has in an equal degree responded to the higher impulses of the age. We possess the loftiest and most various drama in the world—the exponent of sublime and various intellect at epochs of great deeds and thoughts; and to decry the drama as a whole, because some of its component phases have been censurable, is on a par with the prejudices which would banish sculpture, painting, and poetry from the pursuits of Christian men, because there are objectionable statues or licentious pictures and poems.

G

It is accordingly matter of earnest regret to us, to be so frequently assured that our national drama is, at the present moment, on the decline; that it has lost its hold on the intellectual and the refined; that good men denounce it from their pulpits and interdict it to their households; that all is naught in it from Dan to Beersheba; and that a taste for its productions denotes an ill-regulated mind, or a frivolous disposition. We do not propose, in the following remarks upon the present state of the stage and dramatic literature, to meet these objections directly. It will suffice to show what is the actual condition, healthy or unhealthy, declining or advancing, of the British theatre. If we mistake not, while there is much in it to wish otherwise, there is also fair ground for commendation. We shall have done something towards clearing up a vexed and imperfectly understood question, if we can show probable grounds of hope for the future.

It must be owned that the drama labours under many disadvantages at the present moment. We shall not dwell upon their more obvious causes—the habits of social life, the inroads made upon the attractions of the theatre by the counter-attractions of literature, or the ebb of fashion from the stage doors. These disadvantages are on the surface, and a sudden turn in the world's tide would repel and obliterate them. Their sources lie much deeper, and must be sought in the character and tendencies of the age itself.

It is perhaps an inevitable result of advancing civilization, that it levels in great measure the external and salient points of individual character, and thus deprives the drama of one of its principal aliments and attractions. Evil passions and evil natures are unhappily, indeed, the accompaniments of every age, but they do not therefore always exhibit themselves under dramatic forms. The crimes and woes of "old great houses" seldom affect in our days either the annals of the world or the passions of individuals. Wars have lost their chivalric character; politics are no longer tissues of dark intrigues, revealed only by their results, but hidden during their process in impenetrable darkness. Society has ceased to be divided into castes, or distinguished by outward and visible tokens of grandeur or debasement. Our manners and habits have grown similar and unpicturesque. A justice on the bench is no longer worshipful; a squire, except in the eyes of some poaching varlet, is no more "the petty tyrant of his fields;" we take the wall of an alderman, and feel no awe in the presence of a mayor; lords ride in cabs; the coach, with six Flemish horses, with its running footmen and linkbearers, has vanished into infinite space; a knight of the shire may be the son of a scrivener; our men on 'Change have doffed their flat caps and shining shoes; there are no bullies in Paul's Walk, and hardly a Toledan blade within the liberties of London. "The toe of the peasant comes near the heel of the courtier." Our very inns have dropped their pictorial emblems : we write, instead of paint, our tavern-heraldry. Town and country are nearly one. Clarendon says of a certain Earl of Arundel, that " he went rarely to London, because there only he found a greater man than himself, and because at home he was allowed to forget that there was such a man." Lord Arundel's policy would be unavailing now. Our humours and distinctions are wellnigh abolished, and the drama, so far as it depends upon them, is deprived of its daily bread. The stage-poet cannot find his Bobadil in any lodging in Lambeth, nor his Justice Shallow in Gloucestershire, nor Ancient Pistol in Eastcheap. The "portrait of a gentleman or lady" at the Exhibition may represent four-fifths of our similar generation.

Further afield then must our dramatists seek, if they draw from life, for their models of passion and humour. For the most part they suffer no especial inconvenience from the stoppage of supplies, inasmuch as they import them ready-made from the banks of the Seine. We shall advert presently to the number and character of these importations. For the present it suffices to remark, that this assimilation of the external forms of life operates unfavourably upon the drama in two or three directions. It deprives the author of his fund of characters. It renders the audience less apprehensive of individual properties, and more eager for startling

effects upon the scene. The spectator comes to witness in representation something different from what
he sees daily in the streets and markets, in the law-
courts or the drawing-room, and is discontented if
the plot have in it no dash of extravagance, or the
costume and scenery do not blaze with splendour.
The scarcity of healthier food renders him the more
eager for high and artificial condiments. His palate
too has been previously vitiated by the circulating
library. Macbeth is flat after Jack Sheppard; Sir
Anthony Absolute is dull beside Mr. Pickwick. Our
earnestness and our sport have travelled at railway
speed during the present century; and the drama,
like "panting Time," in Johnson's prologue, either
"toils after them in vain," or outstrips them by dint
of surpassing extravagances of story or decoration.

When Sir Roger de Coverley made known his intention of going to the play, the Spectator and Cap-
tain Sentry had no difficulty in discovering at what
theatre that very legitimate drama ' The Distrest
Mother' would be enacted. But a country gentleman of the present day, unacquainted with town—
if, indeed, such a *rara avis* survive in this age of
locomotion—and recurring to his early recollections
of Elliston at Drury Lane, or Kemble at Covent
Garden, would be sorely puzzled at first in his search
for either regular tragedy or comedy. At Covent
Garden he would find Italian Opera installed; at
Drury he might indeed light upon Mr. G. V. Brooke,

"cleaving the general ear;" but he would quite as likely read in the bills of the evening, that a gentleman would walk across the ceiling, or that Franconi's stud would exhibit, or that a second Italian Opera awaited him. At the Haymarket he would witness indeed an excellent comedy of Mr. Planché's, but none of his old favourites, Moreton's, or the younger Colman's, or Reynolds's once popular plays. He would discover that the English Opera House had foregone its name and vocation, and 'Tom and Jerry' given place at the Adelphi to Mr. Taylor's admirable play, 'Two Loves and a Life.' But his amazement would be transcendent on learning that his best chance of meeting with Shakespeare would be in the remote regions where horrors or nautical heroics were wont—"Consule Tullo, in the good days when George the Third was King"—to reign supreme, namely, at the Surrey or Victoria Theatres, beyond the bridges, or at Sadler's Wells, once the Naumachia of our metropolis.

To this Regio Transtiberina of London, indeed, has recently migrated the popularity of the so-called "legitimate drama." Here, and in some of the City theatres and saloons, managers can reckon upon remunerating profits for the production of the 'Tempest' and 'Henry V.,' the 'Duchess of Malfi' and the 'School for Scandal.' Here the check-taker bawls, "Pit full!" and gives the check he takes; here spectators endure five acts, and forbear to vex the manager's brain with

calls for novelties; and here rarely, if ever, penetrate
the last devices of the Porte St. Martin. If the
spirits of defunct managers be permitted at any time
to revisit the glimpses of the moon, that of old J.
Davidge would find matter enough for meditation
upon "mutabilitie." Ariel skims and Prospero stalks
over the boards once dedicated to brigands and midnight murder; and the 'Midsummer Night's Dream'
displays its faery wonders and mortal perplexities
upon the area where British tars fought over again
the battles of the Baltic and the Nile. Johnson
rightly predicted that on the stage of old Drury
"new Hunts might box, and Mahomets might dance;"
but the migration of Shakespeare to Southwark and
Islington was a prodigy beyond the bounds of his
vision.

For these effects, whether defective or not, and
which assuredly are not altogether unfavourable aspects of the drama's condition, many causes may be
assigned. But in order to set them in as clear a
light as possible, whether as symptoms of theatrical
renascence or decline, we shall briefly survey, in the
first place, the representations current at more western
theatres, and in what are esteemed more civilized
regions of the metropolis. And as many of our
readers may be unaware of the number of plays
yearly brought out as novelties, as well as that of
the theatres now open to the public, or the amount
of persons directly or indirectly employed in minis-

tering to them, we think that the following facts
may not be unacceptable :—

In certain recesses of the Palace of St. James, in
Westminster, are annually deposited some hundreds
of manuscripts, the records of gratified or disappointed
expectations. These manuscripts are copies of the
dramas licensed for representation during the preceding twelve months. Of this number not a third finds
its way to the press, or establishes itself in public
favour and remembrance; and of those which are
printed, fewer still survive the year which gave them
birth. It is not, indeed, desirable that there should
be more frequent disinterments from this dramatic
cemetery, since few of its inmates merit a *resurgam*
upon their escutcheon; yet, in the mass, they deserve
some attention, as the abstracts and chronicles of the
theatrical character of the age.

We do not allege these facts as implying any especial reproach either to the authors who produce or
to the public which neglects this class of writings.
Dramatic literature, as regards the majority of its
productions, is, like the art of the actor, ephemeral.
It partakes too much of the passing sentiments or
caprices of the age, and is addressed too entirely to
the eyes and ears of present spectators, to contain,
in general, the germs of perpetuity. If we except
Shakspeare and a few of the greater luminaries of
his age, the elder drama owes its partial immortality
more to its poetic than its dramatic strength. Of

those which linger in the closet, few would be now
endurable on the stage. And at the time these were
novelties nearly the whole imaginative powers of the
English mind were engrossed in the service of the
theatre; whereas, in the present day, with a few exceptions, no poet of any distinction has tried even
his 'prentice hand in dramatic composition. Lyrical
verse has absorbed the most profound and original of
our poetic writers; and the novel has appropriated to
itself the talents which, two centuries ago, would have
been in the pay of Henslowe or Alleyne. It is accordingly less surprising that so few modern plays
should survive their birth-year, than that so many
dramatic writers should be found exerting themselves
in a province of art in which a few weeks of applause
are generally succeeded by irretrievable oblivion.

In the year 1853, two hundred and six dramas
were licensed for representation, and, with very few
exceptions, produced at various metropolitan or provincial theatres; and in that year the number of novelties fell short of the sums of former equal periods.
Of these, the majority were one, two, or at most three
act pieces, the experience of managers or the capa-
bilities of the actors having, we suppose, afforded
grounds for declining the old-established play of five
acts. The precepts of Horace and the practice of
our elder dramatic writers are, indeed, seldom observed by modern poets or critics; and the almost
universal custom of adapting French originals has

tended much to the abbreviation of plots and acts.
Occasionally, indeed, an opposite excess has been attempted, and a *monstrum informe*, in eight or nine
acts, has drawn its slow length through an entire
evening, but the experiment was not so successful as
to be repeated. It would not be easy to classify or
to draw any general conclusions upon the state or
prospects of dramatic literature from these two hundred and six plays. Properly speaking, the elder distinctions of tragedy, comedy, and melodrama, such
as prevailed in the age of the patent theatres, are
nearly extinct. The saloons are still occasionally
chambers of melodramatic horrors, such as once attracted audiences to the Coburg and the Surrey
Theatres. But the passion for volleys of musketry,
and trap-doors, and red and blue lights has much
declined, and with it, in considerable measure also,
the amiable disposition to regard a British tar as an
eminent philanthropist, and the Hounslow brigade as
the redresser of the wrongs of man and the inequa-
lities of wealth and station. On the whole, a considerable improvement both in morals and taste is
apparent even in the theatres where gentlemen may
be seen in the dress-circle unencumbered with coats,
and where the pit, from the prevalence of Israelitish
physiognomy in its rows, exhibits an apparent approach to the restoration of the Jews. The theatre,
indeed, at the present moment, is in more danger
from the social and sentimental corruptions of the

French stage, than from exhibitions of open ruf-
fianism, or the coarser species of vice and crime.
Yet, notwithstanding these partial improvements, the
question whether we possess, or are nearer than formerly to the possession of, a national drama, remains
nearly as far from solution as ever. That dramas
under few obligations, beyond the skill displayed in
their plot and dialogue, to our ingenious neighbours,
can attain popularity, has been proved by the success
of Messrs. Taylor and Reade's plays. But 'Masks
and Faces,' and 'The King's Rival,' and 'Plot and
Passion,' are exceptional instances of merit, and rather
encourage the hope of a restoration of a national
drama, than prove its existence at present. It is
equally curious and mortifying to remark that, in
most cases of the announcement of a new and successful piece, its French parentage is openly avowed,
and credit taken for the skill displayed in its adaptation to a British audience. Nor is it any defence or
palliation of the debt, that our elder dramatists were
equally indebted to Italian or Spanish originals. They
were indebted to Spanish and Italian novels doubtless, though seldom until such novels had passed by
translation into popular belief and favour; but the
dramatic treatment of the stories was original, and
had not been anticipated by the librettos of the Va-
riétés and Porte St. Martin.

The popular drama of the day is accordingly in no
intelligible sense of the term national, but, like so

much of our costume, a Parisian exotic. How does
it fare, on the other hand, with the drama of which
we justly boast, as having surpassed in amplitude of
proportion and in earnestness of feeling, not only the
classic frigidity of Corneille and Racine, but the authentic grandeur and harmony of the great Athenian
masters—with the drama which stimulated the genius
of Alfieri, and filled with wonder and emulation the
far loftier and deeper souls of Goethe and Schiller?
It is our boast, that we are the countrymen of Shakespeare and his contemporaries; but we cannot find or
make them generally attractive on the stage. It is
not for lack of enterprise or accessories; but either
there is some mistake in the application of them, or
the public has been accustomed to a different fare,
and lost its appetite for the diet which it pronounces
to be unrivalled. Never were scene-painters more
expert, or upholsterers more inventive; never was archæology more in request for dramatic illustrations,
or managers more determined to be scrupulous in
costume and landscape. Yet all this avails them
little or nothing—the Mordecai of Parisian "effects"
sits at their gate; and after a brief curiosity about
the ghost of Banquo, or the heraldry of King John,
has been sated, the romantic and historic drama pales
its ineffectual fire before the irresistible attractions
of the 'Corsican Brothers' or 'Janet Pride!' The
public, at least as represented by the press, quarrels
with the managers for corrupting the national taste;

the managers retort on the public, that it cherishes
the corruption of which it complains; and both shift
the blame upon the actors. "Give us," says the
public, "a succession of Kembles, of Keans, or Mac-
readies, and we will dispense with the decorator and
the upholsterer:" "Find us," say the managers, "a
Mrs. Jordan or a Miss O'Neill, and we will spare
ourselves the cost of acres of canvas and galaxies of
light, red and blue:" "Afford us," say the actors,
"equal opportunities for learning and perfecting ourselves in the several departments of our art which our
predecessors enjoyed, and we will prove to you that
the ancient spirit is not dead, but cabined, cribbed,
and confined by the fetters imposed upon it in dramas
which exclude passion, probability, and imitation of
life and manners."

We think that each of the recriminant parties
might make out a very plausible case for itself, which
yet, as a whole, would be an invalid defence. The
public might allege,—We come to your houses for
amusement, and not for a lecture upon scenery, archi-
tecture, and dress. The managers might plead,—We
are engaged in a commercial speculation, no less than
the momentous business of earning a livelihood—we,
who live to please, must please *to* live; and since you
respond to decoration and pomp more readily than to
character and passion, with pomp and decoration we
are fain to provide you. Lastly, the actors might as
fairly urge,—We are clay in the potter's hands; and

so long as you obscure us with light, and dwarf us amid colossal scenery and processions, you render us the secondaries of the stage, and, for any effect we produce, might dispense with us altogether, and expend our salaries upon yet costlier panoramas.

None of these complaints, we are inclined to think, touch the evil complained of. They are, in the first place, vague; and, in the next, they apply equally to the drama of the last century. Since the restoration of monarchy and the theatres, indeed, there has never been a generation in which these or similar murmurs were not audible. Alleyne and Henslowe, and some of their contemporaries, realized respectable fortunes by management, and found performers whom both themselves and their audiences approved. But their lines were set in pleasant places. The habits of social life favoured them : the novel, the newspaper, and the club, the late dinner, and the accomplishments of the world, were not their foe : a morning walk in Paul's, or a morning ride on the great highway of Oxford-street, was followed by an afternoon visit to the Globe or Bull; and if the courtier or the citizen heard the chimes at midnight, the tavern and not the theatre was in fault. We cannot revert to their habits and hours, and must be content to forego with them some of our dramatic spirit. Neither are our theatres, as they were in the age of Anne and the earlier Georges, the resort of statesmen and their supporters for the purpose of political displays and

intrigues. A Chancellor of the Exchequer presenting a purse of gold to Mr. Kean for his defiance of
the Pope in King John, would be a spectacle more remunerating to a manager than the most captivating
importation from the Porte St. Martin; the expe-
dience of Lord John Russell's or Lord Derby's presence in the side boxes for a few minutes in the evening, would lend new radiance even to Mr. Buckstone's
habitual good spirits. We have learnt to separate
business from recreation; and however it may fare
with the former, the theatre has ceased to be an indispensable diversion for our Harleys and Godolphins.
The support of the higher classes is no longer included among managerial anticipations of profit. Her
Majesty, indeed, is a most efficient patron of the drama;
but even court favour is not a counterpoise to the ebb
and recession of " the world " from the dress-boxes.

We doubt however whether, in spite of the abstraction of so important an element, the number of
playgoers has materially declined. We are rather
disposed to think that it corresponds with the greatly
increased sum of our metropolitan population. In
place of some half-dozen theatres, licensed for performance during a few months in the year, and de-
nominated according to their licenses, the winter and
summer theatres, there are now in the Metropolis
twenty-five theatres and saloons, the larger portion of
which are open to the public from October to August.
At the lowest estimate, these establishments find

employment for three thousand persons on their premises, without including the numbers engaged at their
own houses or work-rooms in the various arts of decoration and costume which the stage requires. We
may calculate that the audiences nightly resorting to
these twenty-five houses, amount to five thousand,
without reckoning the extraordinary resort to them
at the seasons of Christmas and Easter, or during
the "first run" of a successful novelty. Our computation will not appear extravagant to any one who
has witnessed the crowds awaiting the opening of the
pit doors of the Adelphi or Princess's Theatres during the earlier performances of the 'Thirst of Gold,'
or 'Faust and Margaret.' We do not, indeed, presume from these facts, that the course of managers
runs with uniform and unprecedented smoothness;
but they afford a fair presumption that we have not
ceased, as is sometimes vaguely asserted, to be a play-
going people. The sum of spectators is distributed
indeed over a wider surface, and particular exchequers
may have been less uniformly replenished; but on the
aggregate there has been an increase,—the theatres,
amid many disturbing influences at work, have not
lacked support.

Amid these adverse influences should be reckoned
the attractions afforded by our numerous literary and
scientific institutions, and the growing popularity of
Shakespearian Readings. If it is good to be amused,
it is better to be instructed; and if the poetic drama

is more justly expounded by Mrs. Fanny Kemble than by any performers now on the boards, it is wiser to resort to her readings than to the theatre. In some degree, both lectures and readings are a compromise between the dramatic instincts inherent in our nature, and conscientious scruples as regards the theatre. The theatre is probably affected by these causes more in the quality than the numbers of its frequenters. They abstract from its benches many of the more intellectual members of society, and thus lessen the demand for a higher and better order of drama. They are not, however, features peculiar to the present age. They are but repetitions of what has already occurred. At Athens the new comedy supplanted its rivals and predecessors, much as the modern drama has supplanted Shakespeare and Racine. Æschylus and Sophocles would no longer draw, or could not find competent representatives; and the Athenian people, who regarded the theatre as a proper object for legislation, passed a law, to the effect that their elder and better drama should thenceforward be read, and not acted, at the Dionysiac festivals. We possess no similar record of the Roman stage. But we know that recitations were as popular at Rome as lectures and readings in London, and that the scale of the theatres and the tyranny of pantomime had, even before the Augustan era, nearly banished the works of Attius and Pacuvius, of Terence and Plautus, from the boards. The preference for lectures and read-

ings may therefore be considered more as an accident
of civilization than as betokening any immediate or
peculiar decadence of the drama.

The inferiority of our actors, again, is a common
topic of complaint; and it frequently proceeds from
persons who have not entered a theatre for years, or
who, like Dr. Smell-fungus, think they manage those
things better in France, and form their notions of
English acting from a rare and supercilious visit to
the boxes on a benefit-night. They reverse, indeed,
the adage, and denounce the unknown as utterly flat
and unprofitable. But so it has ever been. The
players, according to such critics, are always descend-
ing below some fancied standard of excellence. Kemble
lacked the *os magna sonans* of Quin, and was less
graceful than Barry. Quin himself was inferior to
Booth, and Booth to Betterton. In the opinion of
Macklin, Garrick as Sir Harry Wildair came short
of Wilks: in the judgment of Foote, Macklin's Love-
gold was not comparable to Shuter's. Charles Lamb,
whose remarks on acting evince a fine discrimination
of its properties, awards to Bensley a meed of praise
at which the few who remember that sensible but
stiff performer are enforced to smile; and we have
heard veteran play-goers aver, that Mrs. Siddons was
generally inferior in dignity to Mrs. Yates. We
distrust these traditions of vanished perfections, as
we discredit regrets for good old times. They are,
we believe, on a par with Don Guzman's lament in

'Gil Blas' over the decrease of the peaches since his youth. The stage, as a mirror of the times, partakes of their imperfections, as well as of their privileges and merits. Styles of representation, no less than plays themselves, go out of date. That certain kinds of acting were better formerly than now, we have no difficulty in admitting; neither have we now such portraits as Reynolds's, or such eloquence as Burke's. Actors, too, leave behind them their equivalents, not their express images: our grandsires endured no one but King in Sir Peter Teazle and Lord Ogleby; we shall probably see no one equal to Farren. The greedy, credulous, and bragging elders whom Munden so incomparably embodied, no longer exist; the world has grown picked and dainty, and voted them nuisances; and we doubt whether Munden would not now be considered a coarse and improbable actor. Nay, we will go a step further, and surmise that, could we see the original cast of the 'School for Scandal,' some portions of the performance would be not altogether pleasing to our present notions. We have seen the 'Beggar's Opera' degraded from a pungent yet delicate satire upon the Walpoles and Pulteneys to an episode from the Newgate Calendar. Its humour had passed away; its songs had lost their savour; the actors mistook irony for earnest; we seemed to have fallen among thieves, and longed to call for the police, and send them packing to Bow-street. We have felt something of the kind with regard to cer-

tain well-meant revivals of old plays. Their passion
seemed Titanic; the action improbable; the interest
remote; the development too sudden and violent.
Webster's fine tragedy of ' The Duchess of Malfy '
was skilfully adapted to the modern stage and well
acted by Mr. Phelps and his company at Sadler's
Wells in 1851. Yet the effect of it was more strange
and solemn than agreeable. It seemed more germane
to the matter to read of such griefs than to behold
them embodied. It may be, that in an age of material
progress we are become less apprehensive of sad and
stately sorrows, that we look not so passionately into
the mutations of high estate and the graver aspects
of life. Beyond the Shakespearian cycle, indeed, few
of our elder dramas bear revival. Our passion and
our sport are of lighter texture than were those of
our forefathers. But it is a false inference that dramatic sensibility is extinct, because certain kinds of
dramatic composition have ceased to affect us, as well
as that the actor has degenerated, because he, like
ourselves, no longer responds to the wild, solemn,
and preternatural scenes that enthralled our sires two
centuries ago.

From the spectators and the performers we now
pass to the pictorial adjuncts of the drama. With
one and the same breath almost, we demand and decry accuracy of costume and splendour of decoration.
They are indeed ruinous, but they are also indispensable. Like the capricious lover, we can live neither

with them nor without them. We call the managers
who supply them, stage-upholsterers, and taunt the
managers who withhold them for their lack of zeal
on our behalf. 'Richard III.,' unadorned, will not
draw houses; revived with historical illustrations of
dress and scenery—*minima pars est ipsa puella sui.*
Between the Charybdis and Scylla of such verdicts,
the manager should be an adroit pilot to avoid ship-
wrecks.

That the passion for decoration has been burdensome if not ruinous, to managers, and injurious to
actors, we admit—with a protest, however, against its
being reckoned among the peculiar disadvantages of
either at the present moment. This, like the complaint of the inefficiency of the elder drama, is of no
recent origin. It dates as far back as the time of
Dryden, some of whose plays were brought upon the
stage with extreme gorgeousness; it is satirized by
Pope; it was made a subject of reproach to Garrick,
and accounted among the errors of John Kemble.
But it is inconceivable that managers should have
laboured for so long a period under a common delusion—a delusion, too, which militated against their
own interests. Their mistake appears to us to have
consisted more in the indiscriminate employment of
the decorative art than in the art itself. The necessity for ornament is generally in an inverted ratio to
the merits of the piece on which it is expended, even
as the most creative poets stand least in need of the

painter's aid. Rarely are Homer, Shakespeare, or
Dante successfully illustrated by artists, although the
same amount of graphic skill would have been well
employed upon the pages of Rogers, Moore, or Campbell. Passion, provided only it finds competent representatives, will make itself felt; wit and humour,
meeting with fitting exponents, will excite mirthful
responses. So long as Mr. Charles Kemble performed Benedick and Mercutio, it mattered little
whether the scene behind him were an exact representation of a street or garden in Verona or Mantua,
or whether his dress were after the fashion of France
or Italy. The elder Kean attired Othello in a garb
that no nation could claim for its own, yet no dis-
creet adviser would have counselled him to exchange
it for the cumbrous robes of a Venetian magnifico.
We have seen 'The Rivals' performed in a sort of
chance-medley costume — a century intervening between the respective attires of Sir Anthony and Cap-
tain Absolute. We have seen the same comedy
dressed with scrupulous attention to the date of the
wigs and hoops; but we doubt whether, in any essential respect, that excellent play was a gainer by
the increased care and expenditure of the manager.

Excess of decoration has indeed been, in all ages
and nations possessing a national drama, a symptom
and accompaniment of decadence in the histrionic
art. The dramas of Euripides required more sumptuous attire and more complicated mechanism than

the 'Antigone' or the 'Prometheus;' but the plays enacted at the Dionysiac festivals, when Demosthenes was a boy, surpassed in pomp the most gorgeous of the Euripidean repertory. The extravagance of the Alexandrian and Roman theatres is notorious : interminable processions, "maniples of foot and turms of horse," swept across the stage, and the managerial wardrobe would have clad the "senate frequent and full." The Pompeian games offended Cicero by their glare, and Cato by their profusion; but fifty years later, Bathyllus and Pylades would have refused to act in the presence of scenery so common and sordid; and in the age of Claudius and his successor, the stars of pantomime,—the "regular drama" was extinct— played Agamemnon and Achilles in panoplies of solid gold. In the reign of Philip IV., the accoutrements of the Theatre Royal at Madrid were as sumptuous as those of the Viceroy of Arragon, and that too in an age when silver and gold plate were displayed upon the sideboards even of nobles of the third order. Louis XIV. was more economical in his theatrical pleasures; yet a thousand crowns were occasionally expended by him upon a single masque or pastoral at the court-theatre at Versailles—with what advantage to the drama, those inexpressibly tame and tedious productions will satisfactorily prove to any one enterprising or patient enough to read them.

It appears to us that an understanding among the managers of the metropolitan theatres themselves might lead to the saving of much forethought, anxiety, and expense to many of them individually. To such keen rivals, and to a class of men supposed to be sufficiently irritable, it may seem hazardous to suggest the plan of a dramatic congress for the purpose of adopting a classification of theatres. If such a scheme be practicable—and to be practicable it requires only a general consent of the parties interested,—its advantages are obvious. Their various experiences in different regions of the Metropolis, would constitute the materials for a Report upon the condition of the drama. The capacity of the several theatres would afford *data* of the expenses that might be incurred with a fair chance of profit. It would be seen from the particular returns what species of drama is most popular and remunerating in any given neighbourhood. But the principal advantage of such a congress would be the suspension, and perhaps eventually the extinction, of a rash and reckless as well as an unfair system of mutual opposition. The play-bills will illustrate our meaning. Constantly it happens that, when a novelty has proved successful at one theatre, it is adopted, with certain changes—*mutatis mutandis*—at another, although the piece may be peculiarly suited to the house which originally brought it out. It is perhaps impossible to establish a copyright in such cases, because the rival versions of a popular drama, including the earliest in the field, are probably derived from the same Parisian prototype.

Yet even priority of adaptation, and consequently of
risk, ought, in our opinion, to secure priority of profits.
We will cite two recent instances of the invasion of
dramatic property. 'The Corsican Brothers,' in its
English dress, appeared originally at the Princess's
Theatre, and was immediately successful. In the
course of a month there were four or five versions of
the 'Frères Corses,' substantially the same as that
performing at the Princess's Theatre. With 'Sar-
danapalus' the case was even worse. To have produced Byron's play with equally costly accompaniments would have been a hazardous experiment. But
another course was open — to turn the whole into
ridicule; and accordingly burlesques were speedily
produced at the Strand and Adelphi Theatres. Now
we contend that in such procedure there was much
unfairness. The manager of the Princess's Theatre
was, in fact, catering for two rival establishments, and
remunerated by one only. There was no redress:
neither of the burlesques were morally objectionable,
and the public regarded with indifference the scramble
between the rival houses.

We could allege many similar instances of ungenerous competition. The evil, for such we must
consider it, would be met by a better understanding
among the managers themselves, who are the principal sufferers from their own collisions. A "concordat"
such as we have suggested would assign to different
theatres different classes of dramas; the actors would

H

be better classified and better drilled, and the public reap the benefit of special and well-defined performances, elaborated by constant and undivided practice. That such an arrangement is neither impracticable nor visionary is a conclusion warranted by its success wherever it has been partially attempted in this country, as well as by its results where, as in France, it has been long and generally adopted. We do not presume to offer any more particular suggestions—"quod fabrorum est tractent fabri,"—but in further confirmation of our views, we proceed to take a rapid glance at such of our theatres as recently or for some time past have restricted themselves to special classes of dramatic entertainments. We shall have much mistaken the matter, if it can be proved that the comparative prosperity of these houses has not mainly arisen from the judicious limits imposed upon their performances by the managers themselves.

We desire to avoid invidious distinctions; but no one acquainted with the various metropolitan theatres will cavil at our naming* the Lyceum, the Princess's, the Olympic, Sadler's Wells, and the Adelphi, as possessing the best disciplined companies and the most generally accomplished actors of the day. The Lyceum is the home of the vaudeville—we cannot add the English vaudeville, for its productions are for the most part transplanted; their exotic origin does not however affect the merits of their performance

* This article was written in 1854.

and *mise-en-scène*. The Olympic deals with comedies of a higher order, often of native growth, and often, latterly, judicious revivals; but its reproductions, as well as its novelties, form an intermediate class between the old five-act drama and the lighter and more evanescent trifles of the Lyceum. At the Princess's we occasionally have Shakespeare represented with all the pomp and circumstance of modern art, but its stock-pieces are of a more prosaic stamp, of an order midway between tragedy and melodrama, and deficient certainly neither in interest nor dramatic effects. The Adelphi has established a kind of vested property in dramas—genuine Adelphi dramas, in the language of its bills—which may perhaps be most correctly defined as combinations of melodrama with farce. Of Sadler's Wells, as the most popular retreat of the regular drama, we have already spoken; its audiences demand few novelties, and retain the rare faculty of sitting out five-act pieces.

It is, however, less to the particular merits than to the systematic discrimination of these performances that we direct our reader's attention. We believe that the above-enumerated theatres are, from year to year, the most steadily attractive. The spectators know what order of drama they may look for within their walls; the actors are drilled to definite functions, and enjoy the inestimable benefit of playing for many successive seasons together. The decline of the patent theatres was, we believe, principally owing

to their departure from a similar wholesome regimen.
The success of the most remunerative theatres at the
present moment is in great measure due to their resumption of it.   An experiment which, wherever it
has been fairly tried, has proved uniformly salutary,
needs, in our opinion, only a more general application
of it in order to render our national stage as effective
in all its departments as the Parisian.   If the expe-
diency of such a classification were once generally recognized by managers, the inconveniences and unfairness of competition would cease, and the Lord Chamberlain, by granting licenses for distinct classes of
entertainment to the various establishments under his
jurisdiction, would confirm and sustain the improved
organization of theatrical entertainments.   And this,
or some equivalent system of arrangement, has become
the more indispensable as regards the training of the
performers, now that the provinces have nearly ceased
to supply efficient recruits to the metropolitan stage.
In nearly a third of our cities and towns the playhouse is closed : it has been converted into a chapel,
a corn-market, or a lecture-room.   Even where a
manager is enterprising enough to risk a season, it is
usually brief and precarious.   At York, Bath, and
Norwich, at one time the acknowledged nurseries of
the London stage, and which successively sent up
the Kembles, Young, Macready, Liston, Blanchard,
Dowton, and a host of lesser luminaries, the dramatic
campaign ordinarily extended over at least six months

of the year. A London "star" was ably seconded
by provincial satellites, and the latter found no difficulty in keeping pace with the performances at Drury
Lane and Covent Garden. The oldest and most ex-
clusive of the country families regarded periodical
visits to the theatre as much a portion of their social
duties as attendance at Quarter Sessions or an Assize
ball. To be absent from the regular bespeaks of the
High Sheriff or the Members was a mark of eccen-
tricity, or a deficiency in respect to those magnates;
nor was there lacking any interest in the performance
or in the merits of the respective performers. But at
the present moment the High Sheriff might as well
conjure spirits from the deep as expect that an over-
flowing audience will come at his call. A few of his
tenants may gather round their landlord, but his co-
mates and acquaintance are deaf as adders to his summons. Provincial acting is indeed nearly defunct.
The City theatres stand in the place of the provincial
houses; thither popular performers from the Strand
and Haymarket flock as "stars," and there are absorbed the few country celebrities which remain. But
the City theatres are by no means equivalents, as
schools of acting, for their extinct country predecessors. The standard of ability is of a lower kind; the
species of dramas which they represent demand rather
strength of lungs than professional knowledge. The
regular discipline of a respectable country stage—the
discipline that, directed by Tate Wilkinson at York,

and Brunton at Norwich, drilled so many serviceable recruits, both rank and file, for the metropolitan boards—is seldom practised in establishments where rant and buffoonery suffice, and where most of the pieces represented are versions of the newspaper novel, or of third-rate tales from third-rate circulating libraries. Scarcely an instance occurs of a City theatre or saloon supplying the stage with even a tolerable addition to its forces.

We have however said already that we distrust the alleged superiority of the actors of former days, and of the general decline of acting at the present moment. We believe, on the contrary, that, with a better system of co-operation, a single English theatre would rival, in the refinement and effectiveness of its *corps dramatique*, any single Parisian house. We have seen no French comedians, in the same line, better than our incomparable pair of Keeleys. The St. James's Theatre has hitherto imported no performer, with the single exception of Regnier, more variously accomplished or more consummate in skill than Mr. Alfred Wigan; and Mr. Charles Matthews, even in parts more exacting than the usual *répertoire* of the Lyceum vaudeville, has few equals,—we are inclined to add, no superior. It is rarely found that actors excel alike in the lighter humours and the more earnest passions. Garrick and Henderson are perhaps almost solitary exceptions of equal and transcendent merit in Hamlet and Benedick, in Macbeth and Me-

grim, in Richard and Abel Drugger. John Kemble
in comedy, in spite of Lamb's eulogy, was recorded
in his day among "the miseries of human life," and
the elder Kean was absolutely intolerable in the few
attempts he made in the service of Thalia. The present stage however affords an actor who combines
passion with humour in a remarkable degree, and, in
the midst of the ludicrous embarrassments of comedy,
presents us with fervent tragic pathos. No one can
have witnessed the performances of Mr. F. Robson at
the Olympic Theatre, without being struck with the
narrowness of the bounds between sport and earnest.
His farce has a pathetic depth, a grave earnestness,
that touch, at one and the same moment, the sources
of tears and laughter. He is partly Liston and partly
Kean. With less than a cubit added to his stature
Mr. Robson would be among the first Shakespearian
actors of the day. It is unfortunate both for himself
and the spectators that his physical qualifications are
not in better accordance with his dramatic genius.
He lacks presence only to mate Kean in Shylock and
Overreach, or Macready in Virginius and Lear.

Mr. Robson, we believe, at one time obtained considerable repute as an actor in burlesques. He has
fortunately escaped from the evil effects of that most
stupid and barren department of theatrical entertainment. In this censure we do not of course include
such admirable samples of Aristophanic fun as Mr.
Planché so often produces, or Mr. Tom Taylor's 'Dio-

genes and his Lantern.' These are legitimate sketches
of follies as they fly. But the burlesque—which, like
an impure flesh-fly, battens upon the imagination of
Shakespeare or the pathos of Euripides, which avails
itself of the solemn and preternatural machinery of
Macbeth, of the Rembrandt-like picture of the Moor,
of the aberrations of Hamlet, of the revenge of Shylock, of scenes and thoughts the most hallowed among
merely human conceptions, appears to us among the
most despicable products of shallow and heartless
writers, equally devoid of respect for their own age,
or of reverence and gratitude towards their benefac-
tors in past time. Nor are such productions less discreditable to their authors than symptoms of decay
in dramatic art itself. To the spectators the burlesque is noxious, since it accustoms them to associate
the low and the absurd with the sublime and the
earnest; to the actors it is no less injurious, since it
tends to impress them with distrust and disrespect for
their art : nay, by exhausting it upon false and superficial wit, it dulls the edge of legitimate and natural
humour. Nor is the offence at all lessened in our
eyes when the parody is at the expense, not of the
established reputations of the past time, but of contemporary productions of merit. The prospect that
his work may become a butt for ridicule necessarily
renders an author timid and diffident of himself. He
holds his sword like a dancer under the apprehension
that it may soon be struck from his hand by the bat

of a clown. Actors, audiences, and managers are alike interested in stifling these parasitical excrescences of the drama, and in commending the fools that use them to some better vent for their pitiful ambition.

In our brief sketch we have endeavoured to survey the general aspects and conditions of the national drama at the present day. That in some respects it has declined we are obliged to admit; certain species of theatrical entertainment are in abeyance, and probably will not speedily be revived. No great school of actors has succeeded to the Kemble family, and with them the higher order of both tragedy and comedy has expired; few modern plays bear the impress of longevity, and will probably be forgotten before another year has passed away. For these causes of inferiority we have, in great measure, to thank the social character of the age itself; literature supersedes the drama on the one hand, and, on the other, we have opened different sources of instruction and amusement. Yet we do not despond: we believe that the remedy lies in a great degree with the managers themselves. We are persuaded that a more careful elaboration of the means which they possess, a politic division of their forces, an abstinence from unfair and expensive competition, a stricter discipline of their companies, and a more systematic regard to the ethical qualities of their productions, will do much towards winning back to them the educated and intel-

lectual classes of the community. We would not exclude spectacle, but restrict it to theatres where the
space is favourable to gorgeous display. We would
not banish all importations of foreign librettos, but
we would recommend the adaptation of them to our
own social habits and principles. We would borrow
from them, not as dependants, but as pupils willing
to be instructed. We have happily not arrived at an
era of such corruption or degradation as stifled the
theatres of Athens and Rome. With a literature
which still commands respect; with a press un-
shackled, yet for the most part salutarily controlled
by public opinion; with much that is imaginative
and lofty in the character of the age; with an almost
incalculable diffusion of our masculine and harmonious language, we have still a lively and steadfast
faith that the nineteenth century will even yet develope, as among its befitting exponents, an intellectual,
moral, and vigorous national drama.

Our expectations may appear sanguine to the many
who regard the drama as the pastime of an idle hour,
and not as a vital branch of the intellectual life of an
age. We do not ask such persons to affect a spurious
enthusiasm for times which, being more symbolic in
their character, were proportionally more dramatic
also than the present. We would recommend theatrical pedantry as little as ecclesiastical or artistic.
The recreations of the day, as well as its ritual and
its arts, must express contemporary feelings, and not

borrow the exponents of them from past phases of society. Literature has unquestionably borne off many *spolia opima* from the theatre; the material development of the age has given a new direction to its humours and passions; yet, in spite of these abatements, the dramatic spirit is neither dead nor sleeping among us; it has thrown off many encumbrances of stilted diction and spurious sentiment; it has embraced new categories of mirth and earnestness; it has enlisted accessories unknown to our forefathers. In the heart of the chaos which the modern stage too generally exhibits, we possess living germs of a drama that, skilfully trained and organized, may yet become as expressive of the material and intellectual genius of the day as the Sophoclean tragedy was of an ethnic commonwealth, or the romantic play of a Christian monarchy. In developing these materials, authors, managers, and the public, have a common interest; and the first step towards so desirable a change is the recognition, by each in their own sphere and function, of the duty of re-organizing the whole system of theatrical entertainments.

CHARLES KEMBLE.*

ON the morning of the 12th of November, expired, at his residence in Saville Row, Charles Kemble, the last survivor of a triad of artists, whose names are written indelibly in the annals of dramatic art.

The life of an actor, so far as it is an object of public interest, closes with his scenic farewell. The decease of an actor, and especially of one long withdrawn from the stage, might therefore attract little notice at any time beyond the circle of his immediate friends, and at the present moment of anxious anticipation, is more than ordinarily liable to pass from the register of the living with merely a brief expression of regret. Johnson indeed declared that the death of Garrick eclipsed the gaiety of a nation. But this was a friendly hyperbole : the nation laughed or wept as before, although the mighty master no longer touched the chords of its emotions. The actor's task is fulfilled when the curtain descends upon his last impersonation.

* Reprinted from ' Fraser's Magazine,' December 1854.

Yet we are unwilling that the name of Charles Kemble, so long and intimately associated as it has been with the brightest ornaments and the most intellectual age of the drama, should be written on the roll of Death without some accompanying comment and commemoration. The poet, the painter, the sculptor, and the architect, perpetuate *their* fame in their works; but it is the hard condition of the actor that *his* art is for the present only; he has no patent for futurity—neither marble, nor canvas, nor "breathing thoughts and burning words" embalm his genius. With the generation which beheld him, his image and his influence pass away.

We are not in the number of those who regard with indifference the condition of the drama. To a complete and vital civilization it is essential that no province of art should lie fallow and unproductive. If it be desirable that the thought of every age should be embodied in words, colours, marble, or bronze,—if it be important that our material progress should be accompanied by a corresponding moral and intellectual development,—not less desirable and important is it that the drama, which claims from all the arts "suit and service" in their turn, should retain its station among the educational instruments of the age.

But without a great school of actors the drama itself necessarily pines and dwindles. Men capable of casting their thoughts into dramatic forms will not be at the pains to write when none are competent to embody them worthily; and the more cultivated and critical portion of the public abandon the theatre to those who are content with rant, buffoonery, spectacle, and burlesque. That we have still some actors who do honour to their art, and still some authors to supply them with plays worthy to outlive the present, is rather a proof that the ancient spirit is not wholly dead, than of the existence of a generally sound condition of the drama itself. A brief account of one who inherited and transmitted a great name may in some measure illustrate the causes of the former high estate and the present comparative decline of the histrionic art among us.

The youngest by nearly twenty years of a family who for almost three generations formed the central group of all that was excellent on the stage, Charles Kemble was indebted for his eventual position as much to the discipline he underwent as to the dramatic powers which he shared or inherited. Nature had been bountiful to him in its gifts; his form was noble, his features classical and expressive, his voice, although not strong, remarkably melodious. But it was the diligent cultivation of these gifts which finally earned and secured for him his later and mature fame. His brother—who from the difference of their years stood to him also *in loco parentis*—knew well that there is no royal road to histrionic excellence. Hence he imposed upon the young *débutant* a probation as strict

and regular as he was in the habit of prescribing to
the least gifted of his associates. Charles Kemble
was for some years an actor of third and fourth-rate
parts, both in public and professional estimation, and
for many more was entrusted with only secondary
characters. Nor was he an actor who rose rapidly
in public favour. The public compared him unfairly
with his elders; they expected from the incepting
the completeness of the matured actor. The press,
which he never courted, repaid his indifference with
occasional hostility or general silence. He had no
declamatory tricks to catch the unwary; he never
condescended to play *at* either pit or gallery. And
the audience of those days was not easily contented.
Nightly in the habit of witnessing performances of
a high order, their demands were high on all who
aspired to win their favour. There was indeed less
smart newspaper criticism in those days; but there
was instead of it a more competent and formidable
bench of judges in the pit and boxes to probe and
admonish the actor. The audiences of that period
came with comparatively fresh emotions to the theatre. Their sensations had not been blunted by the
semi-dramatic excitement of Byron's poems or Scott's
tales. The novel of that time did not anticipate the
business of the scene. Neither had the men and
women of that time, artificial as were their manners
in many respects, reached that morbid condition of
civilization which now renders the indulgence or ex-

pression of feeling in public little short of a social crime. They went to the theatres to be moved, and they required that the actor should be able to open the sources of their mirth or sorrow. They met him halfway, but they expected that on his part he should be able to evoke the sympathy which they were ready to afford. Nor, at the time when John Kemble and Mrs. Siddons were in the zenith of their fame, did spectators flock to the theatre merely to be moved or amused. The stage was looked upon as a school of manners, as well as the most intellectual of all entertainments. Orators, artists, men of wit and men of fashion, then resorted to Covent Garden or Drury Lane as they now flock to the Opera. To canvass the merits and to attend the representations of English actors was not then considered a token of inferior breeding. It was as legitimate to profess admiration of Shakespeare and Jonson as now of Rossini or Donizetti. *Nous avons changé tout cela*—with what profit appears from the present condition of the English stage.

In such a period as we have sketched, Charles Kemble served his apprenticeship. Behind the curtain his discipline was severe; before it his judges were exacting. But there was a further cause of his final excellence—a cause which hardly survives in the present day. If we compare a sheaf of playbills fifty years old with the present announcements of the theatre, we shall find that in the one case there was a constant repetition of established dramas, in the other there is a rapid succession of novelties. If we examine these documents more minutely, we shall discover also that while the scene-painter and the upholsterer are now at least as important personages as the performers, then the main burden of the play lay on the actors' shoulders. Now the effect of repeating accredited dramas was to render the performer more skilful, to improve his manipulation of character, to concentrate his attention upon the details of his art. To make up for the superficial attractions of novelty he was compelled to give a higher finish to his habitual impersonations. Whatever may have been the demerits of theatrical monopoly, it possessed this inestimable advantage to the actors. They played better individually and collectively. They were animated by a common spirit, and by an emulation not always ungenerous. To sustain the character of the house was no unusual or unworthy ambition.

It appears to us moreover that the elder actors proposed to themselves a different and in some respects a higher standard of art than prevails among their present representatives. They may have been more " mannered," for the age to which they played was more precise and formal. This however was an accident of *their* generation, balanced by other and perhaps less artistic peculiarities in our own. We believe the elder school to have been more ideal. They held fast at least one principle of art of the highest value and moment. They were not content

with a succession of fragmentary efforts; they aimed
at unity of effect; they were not disposed to accept of
occasional bursts of passion as a compensation for
the neglect of the harmony and repose which enter
so largely into every genuine work of art. They esti-
mated the performance on the stage rather by its
total veracity than by its spasmodic and irregular
strength,—even as they would have preferred the
chastised grace of Reynolds to the exuberant and capricious fancy of Turner.

There may have been somewhat too much of
system, too elaborate a display of art, in the declamation of John Kemble; and we whose ears are un-
used to such modulations, and inured if not reconciled
to the harsh and broken tones of modern elocution,
should very possibly be affected with a feeling of surprise if we heard 'Hamlet' or 'Macbeth' so intoned.
Be this as it may, the art of reciting blank verse and
dramatic dialogue generally is among the lost arts of
the stage, and has been supplanted by a trick of enunciation that relieves the dramatic poet from any obli-
gation to write in poetic measures. Throughout his
career, Charles Kemble reflected the influences of his
early discipline. He was, in the first place, a vera-
cious actor, neither adding to nor falling short of the
conceptions of his author. He was moreover a most
industrious and painstaking actor, thinking nothing
done while aught remained to do; inspired with a
high ideal, assiduously striving to reach it, and pro-

bably in his own conception—for such are the feelings of every genuine artist—never wholly attaining it. He loved his vocation with all his mind and with all his strength. He was not one of those actors who regard their efforts as taskwork and rejoice when the mask is laid aside. He highly rated his profession, as one ministrant to the intellect and the heart of man—as at once the mirror and the auxiliary of the poet, the painter, and the sculptor. All his opportunities were made subservient to it—his reading, his travels, his observation of man and man's works, of society, of nature, of contemporary actors native and foreign. In all respects the work he had in hand he wrought diligently. He had none of the petty jealousies of his profession. At the zenith of his reputation he would undertake characters which inferior actors would have declined as derogatory to them. He envied no one; he supplanted and impeded no one. For his art he was often jealous—never for himself. He possessed in an eminent degree the love of excellence; but he was no seeker of pre-eminence. Stanch in maintaining his opinions as to the proper scope and import of acting, he was tolerant of opposition; and prompt in discovering and acknowledging merit in others.

His career as an actor began in one generation and terminated in another. It commenced at Sheffield in 1792, and closed at Covent Garden Theatre in 1840. During that period revolutions took place both in social life and literature which directly and in various ways affected both the form and substance of the drama. Within the first twenty years of the present century a new literature arose, a literature which differed essentially from that of either the sixteenth or the eighteenth centuries. The wits of Queen Anne's reign would have deemed the productions of Byron and Scott as a recurrence to the earlier and ruder periods of Elizabeth; the Elizabethan poets would have regarded them as deficient in earnestness and erudition. As a satirist Byron might have won the applause of Dryden and Pope, and Addison have written a 'Spectator' upon the poetical descriptions in 'Childe Harold.' As a novelist Scott might have ranked with Defoe, and as a poet with Davenant; but the age which admired the 'Grand Cyrus' and 'Clelia' would have little relished 'Waverley' and the 'Heart of Mid-Lothian.' The influence of both these poets was unfavourable to the drama. They supplied the public with sufficient theatrical excitement at the fireside, and weaned them from the theatre by embodying in their writings scenes and sentiments hitherto monopolized by the stage.

They were not the only and perhaps not the greatest poets of their age, but they were the leaders in a species of literature which more than any other has proved prejudicial to the taste for theatrical entertainments. Shelley, Wordsworth, and Keats, and even Rogers and Campbell, were either too limited in their several in-

fluences or too remote and abstract in their genius to
affect materially the public at large; whereas Scott
and Byron embraced and commanded a range of sympathies similar in kind, and nearly commensurate with
the drama itself. Nor was popular literature the only
rival of the theatre. The Continent, long sealed to
Englishmen, was in the fifteenth year of this century
suddenly thrown open to them, and novel forms of art
and untried objects of intellectual interest were pro-
digally afforded to the wealthy and refined classes of
the community. Beside such attractions the theatre
paled and waned. The treasures of statuary, painting,
and music, in their native homes, were simultaneously
thrown open, and the frequenters of the pit and boxes
became travellers by land and sea, and connoisseurs
in arts more intellectual and permanent than any
theatrical show or any actor's impersonation. Nor
must we omit the increased religiosity of the times.
Whether abstract scruples against the stage be well-
founded or not, this is neither the time nor the place
to inquire. But it is certain that the passions and
sentiments of the theatre are frequently such as the
moralist would discourage; and although the actor
may at times be a useful auxiliary to the preacher,
yet his text and his doctrines are not necessarily in
accordance with those of the pulpit. And thus at
nearly the same period these counter-attractions—literature, foreign travel, and religion—combined their
opposite influences against the drama, and drew off
from it myriads of votaries.

But in the year 1792 none of these causes of decline were as yet in operation. Mrs. Siddons, though somewhat past her prime, was still in the full majesty of matronly beauty; and John Kemble stood confessed the legitimate successor of Betterton, Quin, and Barry. Nor, although they were in shape and gesture proudly eminent, were they unsupported. A host of actors, the least accomplished of whom might now be the protagonist at many London theatres, seconded and sustained them—on the spear side, Bensley, Holman, the Palmers, and Barrymore—on the spindle side, Mrs. Powell, Mrs. Crawford, Miss Brunton, etc. In this most high and palmy state of the drama, and before audiences at once susceptible of emotion and skilful in judgment, the younger Kemble made his first appearance in the tragedy of 'Macbeth,' and in the subordinate character of Malcolm.

The earlier impersonations of an actor who rises gradually in his profession are rarely remarked at the time or remembered afterwards. We have however Mr. Boaden's testimony to the "poetry of Charles Kemble's acting" in Guiderius, and his princely demeanour in Malcolm. But it was as the representative of second parts that his powers were first manifested. Those who are old enough to remember the Hamlet, Macbeth, and Coriolanus of his majestic brother; or the Lady Macbeth, Volumnia, and Mrs. Beverley of his matchless sister, will also recall the younger Kemble's chivalrous energy in Macduff, the classical grace of his Aufidius, and the pathos he ingrafted upon Lewson. We do not select these characters as among his best, but merely as illustrations of his powers as an auxiliary to the mature artists of his youthful days. In secondary parts he was indeed at all times unsurpassed, and he continued to perform them long after he occupied the foremost station in the ranks of scenic artists. How full of winning grace and good-humour was his Bassanio, how humorous and true his drunken scene in Cassio, how fraught with noble shame after Othello's dismissal of his "officer"! He was the only Laertes whom it was endurable to see in collision with Hamlet, the only Cromwell worthy of the tears and favour of Wolsey.

We have great pleasure in calling in the evidence of an excellent judge of acting to support our own recollections of Charles Kemble.

" I never" (says Mr. Robson, in his 'Old Play-goer') "saw an actor with more buoyancy of spirit than Charles Kemble; Lewis had wonderful vivacity, airiness, and sparkle, but he was finicking compared with Charles. Who ever played a drunken gentleman as he did? His efforts to pick up his hat in Charles Oakley were the most laughable, the most ridiculous, the most natural that can be imagined. I have seen him perform the character of Friar Tuck, in a dramatic version of Mr. Peacock's ' Maid Marian,' with such an extraordinary abandonment and gusto, that you were forced back to the 'jolly greenwood and the forest bramble.'

He absolutely rollicked through the part, as if he had
lived all his life with Robin and his men, quaffing fat
ale and devouring venison-pasties. But perhaps his
masterpiece in this way was Cassio: the insidious
creeping of the 'devil' upon his senses; the hilarity
of intoxication; the tongue cleaving to the roof of the
mouth, and the lips glued together; the confusion,
the state of *loss of self*, if I may so term it, when he
received the rebuke of Othello, and the wonderful
truthfulness of his getting sober, were beyond de-
scription fine, nay real. No drunken scene I ever
saw on a stage was comparable to it."

But the continued labour, the earnest study, and
unwearied self-examination pursued for many years
were rewarded by greater achievements than these,
and crowned at length with the highest recompense
which an actor can receive for his efforts, viz., that
after witnessing his performance of particular characters, the spectator ever afterwards, even in his
solitary studies and remembrances, embodies the
poet's creations in the very image of the actor himself. The names of Faulconbridge and Mark Antony
instantly evoke the person, the tones, and the looks of
Charles Kemble. In the one we had before us the
express image of the medieval warrior, in the other
that of the Roman triumvir. His Faulconbridge bore
us back to Runnymede and the group of barons bold
who wrested the great charter from the craven John.
His Mark Antony transported us to the Forum and

the Capitol, to the 10th Legion at Pharsalia, to Alexandrian revels, and to the great Actian triumph. "In such characters"—we again appeal to the 'Old Playgoer'—"he just hit the difficult mark. He was noble without bluster; self-possessed without apparent effort; energetic without bombast; elegant without conceit."

With the single exception of Garrick, Charles Kemble played *well*—we emphasize the word because other actors whom we have seen have been ambitious of variety, and imagined they could assume diversified powers when nature had denied them—the widest range of characters on record. If he had no equal in Benedick, neither had he in Jaffier; if his Leon and Don Felix were unsurpassed, so also were his Edgar in 'Lear' and his Leonatus in 'Cymbeline.' He was the most joyous and courteous of Archers, Charles Surfaces, and Rangers. His Jack Absolute was the most gallant of Guardsmen: his Colonel Feignwell a combination of the best high and the best low comedy, as he successively passed through his various assumptions of the Fop, the Antiquary, the Stock-broker, and the Quaker. In young Mirabel again he united the highest comic and tragic powers In the first four acts he revelled in youth, high spirit, and lusty bachelorhood: in the last his scene with the bravoes and the "Red Burgundy" was for its depth of passion equalled alone by Kean's agony and death in Overreach.

I

We should exceed our limits without exhausting
the list of characters in which Charles Kemble had
no equal, and in which, without a combination of the
same personal and intellectual qualities, and the same
strenuous cultivation of them, we shall never look
upon his like again. Slightly changing the arrangement of the words, we take Mr. Hamilton Reynolds's
admirable lines as the fittest expression of our conviction, that with Charles Kemble departed from the
stage the gentleman of high life and the representative of the classic or romantic hero :—

> "We shall never again see the spirit infuse
> Life, life in the gay gallant form of the Muse.
> Through the heroes and lovers of Shakespeare he ran,
> All the soul of the soldier—the heart of the man.

> "We shall never in Cyprus his revels retrace,
> See him stroll into Angiers with indolent grace,
> Or greet him in bonnet at fair Dunsinane,
> Or meet him in moonlit Verona again."

In his provincial engagements at all times, and
latterly on the metropolitan boards, Charles Kemble
performed a range of characters for which his talents
or his temperament were not so well adapted as for
parts of chivalry, sentiment, or comic humour. He
played Shylock, Macbeth, and Othello occasionally,
but not with the marked success of his Hamlet,
Romeo, or Pierre. His performance of this order of
characters arose, latterly at least, from the circumstance that he alone from his position and reputation
was qualified to support in tragedy his accomplished

daughter, on whom had descended the mantle of Mrs. Siddons. But whether it proceeded from his theory of art, or from his peculiar idiosyncrasy, Charles Kemble, so excellent in the representation of sentiment, did not in general answer the demands of passion. His Shylock has been commended by no incompetent judge for "its parental tenderness;" but the infusion of tenderness into Shylock's nature we conceive to have been an error. Shylock may have been attached to Jessica as a wolf to its cub; but if he loved her at all, he loved gold and revenge more; and Shakespeare has, in our opinion, afforded no hint of this palliating virtue in his Jew. On the contrary, in her presence Shylock's language to Jessica is harsh and peremptory; and after she has forsaken him, his lamentations are rather for his ducats and Leah's ring than for his daughter. Again, Mr. Kemble's Moor was certainly of a noble and loving nature, and his form and bearing afforded a good excuse for Desdemona's preference of him to the "curled darlings of her nation." But his Roman features and his elaborate manipulation of the character were not so well suited to the rapid alternations of Othello from absorbing love to consuming anger, from profound tenderness to yet more profound despair, from faith to doubt, from accomplished though erring retribution to overwhelming and fathomless remorse. His impersonation of the Moor was too statuesque, and, beside the quickening spirit of terror and pity which

I 2

Edmund Kean infused into the part, seemed unreal, and was ineffective.

Macbeth again was a character in which Mr. Kemble, if it be compared with his other impersonations, —for we are now contrasting him with himself in various parts,—was less distinguished. Perhaps the recollection of his brother's pre-eminence in the Thane of Fife acted as a drawback upon his own conceptions, and affected him with a kind of despair of rivalry or reproduction. But his performance of it lacked the usual individuality of his historical and heroic parts: his Macbeth was as much " an antique Roman as a Dane;" in his Antony the real man seemed to have revisited the glimpses of the moon; but on the heath, and at the Palace of Scone, the historical veracity was less marked. For the line of characters indeed in which Edmund Kean surpassed all the actors of this century—Othello, Shylock, Richard, Overreach, etc. —Charles Kemble needed certain physical qualifications. The dulcet tones of his voice, which in Romeo and Hamlet went home to the hearts of his audience on the wings of the noble poetry it uttered, were less adapted to convey the trumpet notes, the anguish, and the wail of darker passions. There were also a faintness of colouring in his face and a statuesque repose in his demeanour unfavourable to the sudden transitions and vivid flashes of emotion which such impersonations require. There were perhaps also the corresponding intellectual deficiencies—a want of intensity, vigour, and concentrating power. And, it may be unconsciously, his theory of art led him to disregard too much the occasional demands of the more intense and uncontrollable passions, and to direct his attention rather to the finer and more fleeting shades of character—tenderness, grace, the elaboration of the minor strokes of the picture, and the classic unity of the whole.

Between the impersonations of Kean and Charles Kemble there was a fontal opposition arising from the opposite nature of their respective temperaments. Kean never played a part thoroughly: he disregarded unity altogether—probably he was incapable of forming for himself a complete or harmonious idea of any dramatic character. He acted detached portions alone, but upon these he flung himself with all his mind and soul and strength, moral and physical. For such abrupt and spasmodic efforts he possessed extraordinary physical qualifications. An unrivalled command of sinewy and expressive gesture; eyes that emitted tender or baleful light; a brow and lips that expresed vigour, intensity, and indomitable resolution; and a voice running through the entire gamut of passion, and passing easily from an exquisitely touching tenderness to the harshest dissonance of vehement passion. Hence Kean, who was seldom happy in long-sustained speeches, was incomparable in all striking, sudden, and impulsive passages. Who that ever heard can ever forget the unutterable tenderness of his reply to Desdemona soliciting for Cassio's restoration to favour—"Let him come when he will, I can deny thee nothing:" the blank comfortless despair of his "Farewell the tranquil mind, farewell content!" or the hot tearless agony of his "Oh, Desdemona, away, away!" Who that ever saw them can ever forget his attitude and look—the one graceful as a panther in act to spring, the other deadly as a basilisk prepared to strike—while awaiting the close of Anne of Warwick's clamorous passion of grief: or the glance of Overreach when Marrall turns against him: or the recoil of Luke from his overweening mistress, Lady Frugal: or Shylock's yell of triumph, "A Daniel come to judgment!" or the fascination of his dying eyes in Richard, when, unarmed and wounded to death, his soul seemed yet to fight with Richmond. In recording these gifts—endowments of nature rather than results of study,—we desire to draw and to impress this distinction: (1) That such intellectual and physical qualities as Kean possessed belong to the emotional rather than to the poetical phase of the drama; that the opportunities for their employment are of rare occurrence and are seldom offered except by Shakespeare himself; and that they do not and should not be allowed to supersede the earnest study of human nature, or that mental and bodily discipline which the vocation of the actor demands. (2) That whereas an actor like Kean is extremely limited in his range of parts—the number of his great characters was six or seven at most,—an actor like Charles Kemble, in virtue of his catholic study of art as a whole, of his high general cultivation, of his patient elaboration of details, is enabled to fill with success various and even dissimilar departments of the drama, and to combine in one and the same person the endowments of a great tragic and a great comic actor. The example of Kean would be of little service to any performer not similarly gifted with himself; the example of the Kembles is available even to the humblest members of their profession; and so long as it was followed and held in honour, so long did the stage retain performers capable of doing justice to the classical drama of England.

His performance of Hamlet was perhaps Charles Kemble's highest achievement as an actor. Of the relations which it may have borne to his brother's impersonation of the philosophic prince we cannot speak, but of its superiority to all contemporary Hamlets we entertain no doubt. His form, his voice, his demeanour, his power of expressing sentiment, his profound melancholy, his meditative repose, were all strictly within the range of his physical and intellectual endowments, and had all been anxiously trained up to the highest point of precision and harmony. His performance of this arduous character indeed left nothing to desire except that occasionally the harmony of the execution had been broken by the disturbing forces of passion. Nothing could exceed his picture of loneliness of soul as he stood encircled by the Court of Denmark; what a gleam of joy beamed forth in his welcome of Horatio! now at least he has one faithful counsellor and friend; he is no longer 'all alone. Nothing was ever more exquisite or touching than his "Go on, I follow thee," to the Ghost. Perfect love had cast out fear; faith prevailed over doubt; he will go, if need be, to the bourne of death and the grave: he will dive into the heart of this great mystery, but not in the spirit of despair, or at the summons of revenge, or in bravery, or in stoical defiance, but in the strength and in the whole armour of filial love. We have seen actors who fairly scolded their father's spirit, and others who quailed before it; but, except in Charles Kemble, we have never seen one whose looks and tones accorded with the spirit of that awful revelation of the prison-house and the concealed crime and its required purgation, and expressed at once the sense of woe endured, anticipated, and stretching onward through a whole life. In this scene, so acted, the classic and romantic drama melt into one; it is Orestes hearing the hest of Apollo, and it is the Christian hero, scholar, and soldier standing on the isthmus of time and eternity. Again, in the beautiful scene with Ophelia, in which the great depths of Hamlet's soul are broken up, and madness and love gush forth together like a torrent swollen by storms, with what exquisite tenderness of voice did Charles

Kemble deliver even the harsh and bitter words of
reproach and self-scorning. His forlorn and piteous
look seemed labouring to impart the comfort which
he could not minister to himself. Every mode or
change of expression and intonation came with its
own burden of anguish and despair. Filial love at
one entrance was quite shut out; his mother was for
him no longer a mother; albeit not a Clytemnestra,
yet, like her ($\mu\acute{\eta}\tau\eta\rho$ $\mathring{a}\mu\acute{\eta}\tau\omega\rho$), the wife of an Ægisthus
—no more shelter for the weary on that maternal
bosom; childhood snapt rudely from manhood; the
earliest and holiest fountain of love dried up for ever.
And as yet the dregs of the cup have not been drained.
The love stronger than the love of "forty thousand
brothers" must also be cast off, at least as to all outward seeming; and the arrow which has pierced his
own heart be planted in Ophelia's also. Seeing
Charles Kemble enact this scene we have often marvelled how the Ophelias who played with him resisted
the infection of his grief. But we must not forget, in
thus reviving our recollections of a great artist, that
descriptions of acting are for the most part like pictures to the blind or music to the deaf, or as when a
man beholds his face in a glass, and straightway the
image of it passes away. To those who remember
Charles Kemble's impersonations, and who studied
them with a diligent and reflecting spirit, we shall
appear probably to have traced with feeble lines and
dim colours a portrait whose form and tints are yet

living and fresh in remembrance, and will revive as
often as Shakespeare's pages are laid open. To those
on the other hand who have never witnessed his acting,
we must seem even less expressive, seeking to embody
that which by its proper nature has long ago dislimned
and left not a trace behind. Yet it is much to have
seen even what we cannot delineate to others; and to
convey at least the impression that it was good, harmonious, and beautiful exceedingly. Nor are we unaware that in the foregoing attempts to record our
own impressions we have passed over many examples
of his skill or genius, not less worthy of mention than
those which we have recounted. He restored Mercutio to his proper position as a humorous, high-minded,
and chivalrous gentleman, such as in its most palmy
days maintained the honour of Verona, and figured
in Titian's pictures, or in Villani's pages, ages before
the Spaniard, the Gaul, or the Austrian, pressed down
with armed heel the beauty of "fair Italy." To Petruchio he gave back his self-possession and good-
humour; in Mr. Kemble's hands he was no "ancient
swaggerer," liable to six weeks' imprisonment for his
bullyings and horsewhippings. And neither last nor
least in the catalogue of his impersonations—although
it is the last we can afford space to enumerate—Orlando in Ardennes, the very top and quintessence of
woodland chivalry. Fourteen years have passed away
since Charles Kemble's final retirement from the
stage. Virtually he had withdrawn from his profes-

sion in the winter of 1837, but in the spring of 1840 he consented, at the command of her Majesty, to re-tread for awhile the scenes of his former triumphs. Among other characters he performed, at Covent Garden Theatre, Don Felix, Mercutio, Benedick, and Hamlet. He remained on the boards long enough to witness important changes, if not an absolute decline in the art to which his life had been devoted. He saw its professors, instead of being collected in strong companies, and disciplined and matured by judicious training and collective practice, dispersed over a wide area of theatres, where talents of the first order found no congenial employment, and second-rate actors were able to achieve applause easily. He witnessed the almost entire relegation of the classical drama to theatres which had hitherto been the haunts of melo-drama and buffoonery, and the staple productions of these houses, by an inverse process of migra-tion, transferred to the politer regions of the Metro-polis. He had indeed survived the days of poetic and chivalrous delineation; and himself, the limitary co-lumn of a past age, had come down to the days when the theatres rested their popularity upon plays and plots which combined extravagance of incident with questionable ethics, and the manager relied more upon his scene-painter and his upholsterer than upon his actors. In his younger days Charles Kemble had been approved by audiences composed of the refined, the accomplished, and the judicious; in his latter years

the theatre had ceased to attract these classes generally, because it no longer afforded the means of intellectual entertainment.　We are inclined to think,
at least we would fain hope, that a portion of this
night has passed away.　We possess indeed no longer
well-appointed companies and few actors capable of
answering to the demands of the higher tragedy or
comedy.　But we have among us, though still dispersed, and thereby deprived of the advantages of co-
operation, no inconsiderable number of accomplished
actors, who would, in their degrees, have earned themselves a name in any period of the stage-history.　We
have play-writers, too, though their number be small,
who, inspired with an honest purpose, may yet do
much at once to improve the actor in his art, and
elevate the audience in their taste and perceptions.

We should not be rendering full justice to the memory of Charles Kemble were we to omit mentioning
his exertions in the cause of the historical drama by
restoring to it, or affording it for the first time, its
proper scenery and costume.　His brother had expunged much of the neglect and barbarism in these
matters which had disgraced the stage of Betterton,
Quin, and Garrick.　He had rescued Othello from
his footman's garb, Macbeth from his brigadier's
uniform, and Brutus and Coriolanus from their surplices and slippers.　But the younger Kemble went
many steps further; and in his representations of the
Moor of Venice, King John, and Henry IV., put upon

the stage the senators and captains of the Signory,
and the Barons of England, even in the very garb
worn by them when their Dukes wedded the Adriatic,
or Hotspur and Worcester fought at Shrewsbury.
His "revivals" have indeed been eclipsed; but the
drama owed as much to Charles Kemble a generation ago, as it now owes, for the splendour and propriety of its historical accompaniments, to Mr. Macready, Mr. Phelps, or even Mr. Charles Kean.

Hitherto we have considered Charles Kemble in
his public capacity alone; but he was too remarkable
as a man and as a member of refined and intellectual
society to be regarded merely under his aspects as an
actor. In our account of him in his professional relations we have indeed anticipated many of his individual qualities. His intellectual powers are presumed
in his ability to conceive and impersonate the highest
order of dramatic character; he who is competent to
embody poetic creations must necessarily possess no
ordinary share of the imaginative faculty itself. He
who is able to analyze, combine, and reproduce the
fine and subtle elements of Shakespearian life, cannot
have studied either universal or specific human nature
with an unlearned eye, without exerting, and that in
no common degree, the perceptive and logical powers
of the understanding. His fine and cultivated taste
was displayed in the grace of his manners, in his noble
demeanour, and in the skill with which he enlisted
the arts in the service of the drama. But apart from

bis profession, Charles Kemble's acquirements in literature were considerable. He spoke fluently and
with elegance several modern languages ; he was well
versed in the masterpieces of their literature. Although not perhaps a deep classical scholar, he was
familiar with the best writers of ancient Rome ; and
as the amusement of his declining years and comparative seclusion, he renewed his early knowledge of
Greek, and prosecuted its difficult study with the zeal
and energy of an aspirant for University honours.
Like his brother, and indeed like his family generally,
he derived from nature linguistic faculties of the first
quality. Had John Kemble not been the greatest
actor of his day, he would most probably have been
among its very foremost philologists, as the notes he
has left upon the subjects of his various reading abundantly evince. And these philological powers were
shared by his brother. The labour he bestowed upon
the technicalities of the Greek grammar was to him
a labour of love. With half the amount of toil he expended upon the dry, and to most people intolerably
minute, details of its accidence, he might have at-
tained facility in reading Homer, Xenophon, or Euripides. But he would dive to the very roots before he
indulged in the luxury of the fruit or flowers; and a certain air of abstraction observable in his looks, was often
owing to the circumstance that, in his walks or while
seemingly unoccupied, he was carefully going through
in his memory some knotty *paradigma,* or defining

for the twentieth time the precise import of the Greek particles. Art, and the department of sculpture especially, he had made the subject of earnest study—in some measure perhaps as auxiliary to his own profession, but also from more catholic and higher notions. Winckelmann himself might have been proud of a pupil who appreciated the beauty of ancient sculpture with a zest and discernment scarcely inferior to his own. In both his literary and artistic acquirements, Charles Kemble's sphere of observation had been greatly enlarged by extensive travels—at a time when travelling was neither so usual nor so easy as it has since become—and by constant communication with intelligent and accomplished artists, British and foreign. His house indeed was at all times the resort of persons distinguished in art and literature; and rarely did they encounter a host more capable of estimating their common or particular excellencies, or who entered with a more cordial interest into their respective pursuits.

Distinguished by a courtesy of demeanour, even in days more courteous than our own, Charles Kemble transmitted to the present age the express image of the English gentleman of the past generation—of the gentlemen whom Reynolds painted, and of whom Beauclerc was the sample and representative. He was indeed not less formed to delight and instruct private society than to be the mould of high breeding and the glass of refined manners on the stage. In his later years his own social enjoyments were much impeded by deafness, and by the recurrence of a painful disorder. But neither privation nor pain diminished the urbanity of his address or the general sweetness and serenity of his temper. With a shrewd perception of character, he was lenient in his judgment of men and their opinions. He was slow to censure and swift to forgive; and more inclined to make allowance for error than prone to detect imperfections.

In the long period of days allotted to him, Charles Kemble had both mingled much in society and marked its features with a learned eye. His fund of anecdotes was inexhaustible, and his stories derived as much grace and point from his mode of relating them as from their intrinsic pith and moment. It is much to be regretted that he did not write a volume of reminiscences. The arc of his experience stretched from the days of Burke and Sheridan to the present moment; for at every period of his life he had sought the society of his elders and courted the intimacy of men younger than himself.

Charles Kemble has departed from us in the fulness of days, and attended by the respectful affection of a numerous circle of friends. His name will endure as long as the records of the stage retain their interest, and wherever the genius of the actor is held in honour. But it is the condition, twin-born with the nature of his powers and the demands of his art, that he who in his day reaps the first harvest of popularity,

is, after that day has passed, the soonest forgotten in
all but—Name. Yet he is not without compensation
for the ephemeral nature of his efforts and triumphs.
If neither the pencil nor the chisel have power to
perpetuate the effects which once electrified multitudes—if the flashes of his genius be

> " All perishable; like the electric fire,
> They strike the frame, and as they strike expire:
> Incense too pure a bodied flame to bear,
> Its perfume charms the sense, then blends with air;"

yet, on the other hand, while the painter, the sculptor,
and the poet are generally compelled to expect from
the future their full meed of honour, the recompense
of the actor is awarded to himself; he enjoys the
fulness of his fame, and is at once the inheritor and
witness of his own triumphs. To no one but the
actor is it given to speak at once to so many feelings, to move and permeate so vast a mass of human
passions; to impart pleasure, enlightenment, and instruction to so many delighted auditors. He is the
interpreter of the arts to the many: he holds the keys
of sorrow and mirth. It is his voice, or gesture, or
look, which has filled the eyes of crowded spectators
with gentle tears, or has elicited from them bursts of
genial laughter. But for him, poetry might have
been dumb and painting meaningless to many men
and many minds. He is the merchant who brings
the gold of Ophir and eastern balsams within reach
of those whose abode is far removed from the regions

where Nature has exerted her most subtil and strange alchemy.

The place of Charles Kemble in his profession, though long vacant, has never been supplied; nor is it probable that it ever will, for he combined in an unusual proportion intellectual powers with natural gifts; the void which his decease has made in the circle of his friends is as little likely to be filled up, for he united all that is pleasant in man with principles and virtues of "sterner stuff." In contributing our mite to the final *Plaudite* of Charles Kemble we will repeat the challenge of the greatest orator of Rome, uttered upon the decease of Rome's greatest actor: " *Quis nostrûm tam animo agresti ac duro fuit ut Roscii morte nuper non commoveretur? qui cum esset senex mortuus, tamen propter excellentem artem ac venustatem videbatur omnino mori non debuisse.*"

THE DRAMA, PAST AND PRESENT.*

———◆———

THE production of one of Shakespeare's plays with all the accessories of modern decoration, has become almost an annual event at the Princess's and Sadler's Wells Theatres. The late winter season did not exhaust the attractions of 'Pericles,' and the present summer season will probably expire before 'Henry VIII.' has ceased to "draw." We do not profess to know whether the speculation is a remunerative one to the respective managers of those theatres, nor do we indeed wish to combine calculation of profits either with the laudable enterprise of Mr. Kean and Mr. Phelps, or with the great dramas which they present yearly to the public. We trust that they are duly compensated for their pains, risk, and cost; such labourers are fully worthy of their hire. Whether these representations be remunerative or not, they are highly honourable to both these gentlemen, and entitle them to a name and station among

* Reprinted from 'Fraser's Magazine,' July 1855.

the ablest and most intellectual conductors of our National Drama.

We propose to regard this annual event from a more independent point of view than the mere theatrical interests involved in it. It is, if it has any significance, a test of the dramatic character of the age itself. For each reproduction suggests the question, Do the managers employ all this care and cost upon Shakespeare because the public regard him as the roof and crown of dramatic poets, or because, from the historical interest and amplitude of his plays, they coincide better than any inferior creations of the playwright with the present taste for scenical pomp and circumstance? On this issue rests the main question of Shakespearian revivals.

We will commence with the earlier of the present year's Shakespearian representations. The purely dramatical interest of 'Pericles, Prince of Tyre,' is inferior to its poetical merits. It is less a play than a superb romance in dramatic form. It has been suggested, and we think with great probability, that Shakespeare, in this late child of his ever-teeming fancy, was making an experiment upon some new and untried species of dramatic poetry,—a species which should more intimately combine than had ever been done before the romantic with the classical drama. As regards the scene, it is laid almost entirely in that rich and beautiful region which connects Europe with Asia, and which listened to the first articulate sounds of the Grecian Muse.   As regards the characters, they present themselves under Greek designations, yet with the attributes of chivalry and romance. Pericles is a Greek Paladin ; he is the successful champion at a tournament, not the victor at Pythian or Olympic games; he worships indeed in the temple, and consults the Oracle of the Ephesian Diana, but his sentiments are those of a Christian knight, and his deeds resemble those of the heroes of the ' Mort d'Arthur,' rather than those of the Iliad.   To what great issues Shakespeare might eventually have wrought dramas of the Periclean kind we cannot tell.   It is his first and only essay in this species; and it differs essentially from his other historical plays, whether derived from English or Roman annals.

This composite character however renders ' Pericles' less effective as an acting play.   The story does not culminate strongly nor rapidly : a more than usual license is taken by the poet as regards space and time; and, properly speaking, it is rather a series of dramas connected by the principal character, than a dramatic action with its rightful origin, progress, and *dénoûment*.   ' Pericles' indeed is not much unlike one of Plutarch's Lives put on the stage.   In proportion however to its romantic rather than its dramatic qualities was its fitness for decoration.   We have never witnessed any representation in which the adjuncts of the scene were so completely justified and in place.   They did not overlay nor interfere with the proper action of the piece; the acting indeed melted itself into the spectacle, and formed with it an harmonious whole. The indwelling soul of the poetry was sensibly felt throughout as sustaining but not impeded by its pictorial accompaniment. It scarcely mattered whether the declamation of the verse were good or bad; there was a noble picture with a still nobler comment; never, in our opinion, have the modern resources of decoration been more appropriately employed than on this drama. The eye was charmed, even if the heart were not touched, by the spectacle presented to it.

With the latter Shakespearian representation at the Princess's, the case is altogether reversed, and the question again arises—how far the historical plays of the poet are illustrated or encumbered by the art of the painter and the dress-maker. Before however we enter upon this question, we must pay our tribute to the manager for having omitted nothing which it was in his power to obtain and present in the way of adjunct. Regarded as a spectacle, 'Henry VIII.' as represented at the Princess's Theatre, is deserving all praise. The scenery, costume, and groupings are equally correct and beautiful, and this noble drama, so far as regards its accessories, has never been so worthily represented.

The so-called trial scene of this play is familiar to many who have never witnessed a representation of it, through Harlowe's celebrated picture of Mrs.

Siddons and John Kemble as the Queen and the Cardinal. Mr. Kean however has given a more correct representation of the Court as it really sat. In the picture, the King presides and the Cardinals sit below the steps of the royal dais. On the stage, at the Princess's Theatre, the Cardinals, as Lords of Appeal, more properly occupy the higher seat, while Henry and Katharine, as appellant and respondent, occupy chairs to the right and left of the consistorial throne. This is a decided improvement on the former arrangement; but we are not disposed to be equally content with the substitution of a panoramic view of the Thames, from the Palace of Westminster to Woolwich, for the animated scene in the Council-chamber, where the sturdy King rebukes the smooth-tongued Bishop of Winchester. As the representative of bluff King Hal was by no means incompetent to the character, we cannot understand the policy of this retrenchment. It is a costly sacrifice to mere spectacular effect.

But the very skill and happiness with which this drama has been set upon the stage suggests the question, whether there remains sufficient appreciation in the audiences of the day for the higher forms of the drama, apart from the pomp and circumstance of decoration. And 'Henry VIII.' is a fair test of the relations between a taste for the drama and a mere relish for its accessories. We are not aware whether, before Mr. Phelps was hardy enough to make the at-

tempt, ' Pericles' had ever been represented. Be that
as it may, that drama was most effectually aided by
the frame in which it was exhibited. But ' Henry
VIII.' has been so frequently enacted as to deserve
the appellation of a " stock-piece." It was performed
by Macready, Young, Henderson, and Kemble, with
all due attention to historical circumstance and costume, though with less scrupulous care than Mr.
Kean has now bestowed upon it. It was enacted
by Garrick's and Betterton's companies with no
thought of propriety at all, and its original representation was probably even still more rude. Yet,
under all circumstances, ' Henry VIII.' has been a
favourite with the public, whether it has been aided
by the scene-painter and the antiquary, or whether it
has been left to the uninformed caprice of the manager and the contents of the property-room. We may
therefore ask fairly, whether the play owes its present
attractions to the splendour and appropriateness of its
scenery and dresses, or whether unadorned it would
have proved equally acceptable to the spectators who
now throng to it ?

Of all the historical plays of Shakespeare, ' Henry
VIII.' is perhaps the one which in the highest degree
justifies and rewards the modern passion for decoration. The entire scene of the drama lies in the court
and palace of the King. Its actors are the supreme
rulers, pontiffs, and magnates of the land, therein resembling most nearly the first play of the historical

series, 'King John.' Moreover, the Court and age of the Tudors was unprecedented in their pomp and splendour. It was a royal, a feudal, and a learned age combined in one. There was however a marked difference between its royalty, feudality, and learning, and those of the era of Richard II. Under that feeble but by no means illiterate monarch, the lighter graces of literature were in vogue. Chaucer and Gower and Froissart were among the king's favourites: they presented him with their amatory and courtly verses— with their romantic and chivalrous tales. But the Muses of the Tudor Court were altogether of a graver mood. Wyatt and Surrey had imbibed the tender melancholy of Petrarch more than the mingled humour and pathos of Boccaccio, and these "sad poets" by no means represented the fashionable learning of their day. The King was a school-divine; the solemn and sonorous language of Rome was the common language of authors. Henry relished a theological quarrel as fully as he did a wrestling-match or the bear-garden: his advisers were cardinals and archbishops; he did not shrink from the subtleties of the schoolmen, or the canon-law. All around him, from the conclave to the masque, was full of state and solemnity; and the wealth which his father had bequeathed, or which the spoil of the monasteries afforded him, was lavished upon external adornments.

Schlegel has carelessly asserted that "'Henry VIII.' has somewhat of a prosaic appearance." Had the critic

K

ever read attentively the "Prologue" to the drama?
The author therein indicates no prosaic intention;
on the contrary, he prepares his audience for unusual
stateliness and passion. He excludes the comic adjuncts of the dramas immediately preceding. He
professes an almost historical veracity: he proclaims
that he is about to make unwonted demands upon
their pity.

> " I come no more to make you laugh : things now
> That bear a weighty and a serious brow,
> Sad, high, and working, full of state and woe,
> Such noble scenes as cause the eye to flow,
> We now present. . . .
> Therefore, for goodness' sake, as you are known
> The first and happiest hearers of the town,
> Be sad, as we would make ye : think ye see
> The very persons of our noble story
> As they were living ; think you see them great,
> And followed with the general throng and sweat
> Of thousand friends ; then, in a moment, see
> How soon the mightiness meets misery !
> And if you can be merry then, I 'll say,
> A man may weep upon his wedding-day."

This surely is no preparation for " a prosaic " tragedy. The excellent critic indeed seems to have
nodded before he had completed his survey of the
great round and compass of Shakespeare's historical
tragedies.

Let us examine for a moment the entire arch of
Shakespeare's historical drama. The consideration
of the series will enable us to understand better the
actual and the relative position of ' Henry VIII.'

In 'King John,' feudalism and the Church are the assessors if not the co-rivals of the monarchy. The crown is but an ampler coronet: the King trembles before the words of a priest. The public and warlike events of the time are set forth with solemn pomp, the better to conceal a central void of corruption. The King, though royal in his bearing, is essentially false and mean in his nature, and would be utterly contemptible did he stand alone in his baseness. But his brother-monarch is little less insincere than himself; and the nobles, lay and clerical, are little better than this pair of kings. William Longsword alone exhibits the qualities of a true nobleman; he alone takes no part in the hollow truce; he alone remains by the side of Constance on her throne of sorrow. Of this maze of intrigue, Faulconbridge is the chorus and interpreter. He neither possesses, nor affects to possess, high principles; his fortune is to be made; he has gained one step by accepting the bar sinister as a Plantagenet: he looks to ascend higher by playing off one gamester against another. Commodity, as he candidly informs us, is his lord, and he will worship it; and we respect his candour, though we cannot say much for his disinterestedness.

In this the earliest in the chronological order of history, though not of composition, among Shakespeare's historical plays, we are made to feel the existence of a power superior to both the throne and the factions of the nobles. The banner of the Church

is still in the van of earthly policies, prompts or se-
conds every temporal intrigue, and is the gainer in
every collision. In 'Henry VIII.' the Church, at
first splendid and triumphant, is in the end van-
quished and humiliated; in 'King John' her authority is paramount, and disobedience to her hests, whether by the English or French, is followed by defeat
and disgrace.

In 'Richard II.' we encounter a new phase of monarchy. The spiritual power is altogether in the back-
ground, not because her might has already waned,
but because the controversy in hand needs not her
interference. More than one hundred years have
elapsed since the reign of John. In that interval the
power of the nobles has been enfeebled, a succession
of victories over the French and the Scots have rendered the Crown popular, and the wearer of it feels so
confident in his title and his strength, that he can
afford recklessly to gamble both of them away. The
catastrophe and the moral compensation are produced
as much by an inward change in Richard himself, as
by external events. Amid all his follies and extravagances he has a noble kingly nature, awaiting only
the purification of sorrow to resume its original lustre.
He has profoundly disgusted his nobles; he has cut
away the props of his throne; nor until it is tottering
beneath him does he become aware of the dignity or
duties of his station, or eager for either the love or
respect of his people. Nor does he fall so much by

violence as by fraud. The usurpation of the crown
has been long completed before it is publicly avowed.
Bolingbroke acts as a king, and his adherents regard
him as such, although all the while he bruits it abroad
that he has returned from exile merely to demand his
birthright, and the removal of abuses. The feudal
brilliance of the age, so prominent in ' King John,' is
displayed in ' Richard II.' in the earlier scenes alone.
After that bright and stirring dawn the day is over-
cast, and sets in grief and masterless passion.

The key-note which is sounded in the first play of
this historical series is scarcely audible again in the
trilogy devoted to the life and acts of Henry V.,—
for that monarch is evidently Shakespeare's favourite
hero in English history, and the principal character
of the dramas in which he appears. The ecclesiastical
power in these plays, as well as in the earlier-written
triad of ' Henry VI.,' is little more than the instrument of the secular, and has little state or dignity of
its own.   In ' Richard III.,' again, the stir and strife
of the great feudal houses are on the wane.   The old
aristocracy is jealously combating with the upstart
nobility of the Woodvilles, and the last heir of the
princely line of York serves his faction, no less than
his own ambition, by bringing them to the block.   A
reign is then passed over, for although Ford, in his
' Perkin Warbeck' has skilfully selected one episode
from it as suited to the stage, the general sway of
Henry VII. was too peaceable and merely political

to afford proper nutriment for the historical drama. With the accession of his son, however, a new epoch begins, an epoch springing in lusty youth and vigour from the prosaic level of the preceding reign. The civil wars were at an end; the present heir of the Red and the White Roses was unquestioned in his title to the throne; the territorial magnates had become a court *noblesse*, and Henry VIII., under the politic guidance of his Cardinal minister, combined almost despotic power with a large measure of his people's love.

As the conclusion of this unrivalled series of history in dramatic form, we may expect to find in 'Henry VIII.' a repetition and resumption of the main elements of the preceding plays. If we are right in conjecturing that the poet intended to connect them by some common and pervading features, the harmony of art will require that between the first and the last there shall be some points of near relation, as well as of direct antagonism. And accordingly we find both affinity and opposition in 'King John' and in 'Henry VIII.' The King is no longer ruled by the Church, but he rules through an ecclesiastic; the nobles are no longer at variance with the Crown, but cluster around and contribute to its splendour. The old feuds indeed have not burned out. The old nobility cannot stomach the *parvenu* Wolsey; the lay lords are impatient of the influence of the spiritual; and the latter enlist in their ser-

vice men whom they have raised from obscurity.
For the first time also in this historical panorama,
we meet with the Commons of England; not indeed
distinctly limned, yet not obscurely indicated.   In
' Henry VI.' we have Jack Cade only, and his Jac-
querie.   Bolingbroke indeed doffs his bonnet to the
multitude, but it is with Absalom's purpose of winning adherents.   But Henry IV. was raised to the
throne by the Percies and Worcesters, and not by
their untitled adherents; and Richard III. courts the
citizens of London rather that he may have the
pretext of a popular cry in his favour than because
the voice of the Common Hall was as powerful as his
men-at-arms.   In ' Henry VIII.' however we hear of
the "grieved Commons;" of oppressive taxation; of
grinding Commissions; of dangers from popular dis-
content; of unmannerly language—

> " Such which breaks
> The sides of loyalty, and almost appears
> In loud rebellion."

Perhaps the plastic power and tact of Shakespeare
are more conspicuous in this than in any other play
of the historical series.   Its elements, to any inferior
hand, are ungenial.   No great controversy is involved
in its action, like that of the Roses ; no overwhelming
catastrophe, like that of ' King John' or 'Richard II.;'
no sudden metamorphosis, like that of ' Henry V.;'
no fierce Machiavellian spirit, informing the whole,
as in ' Richard III.'   The comic element is nearly

excluded : the fall of Buckingham and of Wolsey, the
wrongs of Katharine, are not relieved by glimpses of
the squirearchy of Gloucestershire, or revellings at
the Boar's Head in Eastcheap. The incidents indeed
are juridical. Buckingham is tried by the Court of
High Commission, and convicted on the evidence of
his steward; Wolsey's ruin is wrought partly by the
King's wrath at the law's delay, and partly by the
King's passion for Anne Boleyn; and Katharine is
discrowned on a plea cognizable by the Court of
Arches. Yet the leaden ore of 'Hall's Chronicle,'
from which Shakespeare has mainly derived his dramatic incidents, is transmuted by his potent elixir
into gold as unalloyed as that of the 'Midsummer
Night's Dream.' He has turned to the highest poetry
the prosaic dealings of courts and the world. And
his tact is the more admirable from the circumstance
that Queen Elizabeth was among the spectators of
the play. There was much offence in the matter, if
not strictly looked to, and wisely handled. On the
one hand dramatic truth and consistency were to be
preserved, on the other the royal anger was to be
dreaded. Yet, by the royal bearing of Henry, by his
festivity, his reliance at first on Wolsey, afterwards
on Cranmer; his readiness to redress the Commons'
grievances, and his show of justice in curbing the
pride and retrenching the power of the Cardinal—he
has produced a picture which even a daughter could
applaud. Nevertheless, to the intelligent observer, he

has drawn Henry as faithfully as Holbein himself. He has represented him as he was actually: haughty and self-willed, voluptuous and unfeeling; capricious alike in bestowing and in revoking favours; possessing a rude sense of justice, and often only revengeful when affecting to be just. He has enlisted our entire sympathy for the victims,—for Buckingham, the Queen, and even the Cardinal: he has kept out of sight the fatal vanity of Anne Boleyn, and represented her as irresistibly beautiful, and yet as regards her ill-fated mistress perfectly blameless. Finally, after the tragic passion of the scene has passed away, and "poor Edward Bohun," and Wolsey, and the Queen, are released from their earthly career, he has imparted to this sad and stately drama a hopeful and triumphant close. Cranmer, the representative of the new opinions, connects the era of Henry with that of Elizabeth, and although his prophetic vision of the great Queen's reign is not penned by Shakespeare's hand, there is enough in his own unquestioned work to suggest the proper consummation.

With an opulence peculiar to himself, Shakespeare, in fact, in ' Henry VIII.,' has included and interwoven three tragical stories,—the fall of Buckingham, the fall of Wolsey, and the more lingering death of Katharine. Of these, the fall of Wolsey, and not, as Schlegel has stated, the calamities of the Queen, is the central object of the group. The Cardinal smites with a two-edged axe. Buckingham and Katharine have each thwarted and offended him: the former he strikes down by show of justice and real subornation; against the latter he sets in action the machinery of the divorce. But this weapon also is two-edged, and the great Cardinal is himself struck down by it as soon as it has served his purpose with his victims.

In contemplating the play itself we have been carried away from its present representation. It would be interesting, were it possible, to arrive at some conception of the effect of this drama upon spectators who lived before the days of theatrical decoration. It requires little stretch of the fancy to conceive 'Henry VIII.' enacted in the court-dresses of George II., or in the more picturesque costume of the preceding century. Cato's flowered gown and lackered chair served as well for English as for Roman dramas. The age had not grown "picked and curious;" and was content to see the players in the ordinary garb of well-dressed "persons of quality." But it does require some power of imagination to realize a play so capable of scenical illustration, performed with no other adjuncts than tapestry hangings, and on stages little larger than the platform of an ordinary lecture-room. The managers of the year 1600 might very probably afford priests' vestments for Wolsey and Cranmer, and farthingales for the beardless boys who "voiced" Katharine and Anne Boleyn at the Globe or Bull theatres. But they assuredly were not

at the pains to dress Henry after Holbein's portrait,
nor to observe a difference between the costume of
Surrey and the Lord Chamberlain. Nor have we,
as in some others of Shakespeare's historical dramas,
any clue among the explanations of the chorus to
guide us. From the chorus to 'Henry V.', as well
as from an often-cited passage of Sir Philip Sidney's
'Defence of Poesy,' we may form an adequate no-
tion of the rudeness of these early representations.
Shakespeare's Prologues are indeed well worth the
attention of modern managers. Those in 'Henry V.'
especially, unite epic pomp and solemnity with lyrical
earnestness, and are intended to remind the spectators that the grandeur of the actions described cannot be developed on a narrow stage, and that they
must therefore supply from their own imaginations
the deficiencies of the representation.

> "Four or five most vile and ragged foils,
> Right ill disposed in brawl ridiculous,
> Disgraced the name of Agincourt."

'Henry VIII.' was doubtless as inadequately represented as 'Henry V.,' and the fancy of the spectators was held in full play through the poverty, or
rather through the absence, of decoration.

Of such poverty we have no longer to complain,
and perhaps have more reason to murmur at our present opulence. For if we in reality succeed in exhi-
biting the tumult of a great battle, the storming of a
fort, the splendour of a council-chamber, or the pomp

of an ecclesiastical procession, we incur the opposite
risk of rendering the spectator, by the power of these
sensible impressions, indifferent to the proper business
of the scene and those who move upon it.   The essential is sacrificed to the accessory.   In this respect
however the public and the managers have long since
combined to spoil each other: the one by demanding,
the other by supplying ornament in excess, as the
proper instrument of dramatic attraction.   Whether
Timotheus should yield the prize, or both divide the
blame, is a question which cannot be discussed within
our present limits.

It has for some time been a fancy of periodical
critics to denounce managers of theatres as the worst
enemies of the dramatic poet.   They ring interminable
changes on translations from the French, on the sacrifice of genius to stage convenience, on the subordi-
nation of the play-writer to the servants and hand-
maidens of the scene, and on the jealous exclusion of
dramas which do not, or cannot, directly minister to
public caprice or managerial profit.   From the specimens recently afforded of the modern poetical drama,
we are disposed to think that a very slender proportion of genuine dramatic ability is excluded from the
theatre; and in short, that managers exercise a sound
discretion for the most part in rejecting the wares
presented to them.   Without regarding these gentlemen as judges from whom there is no appeal, we believe they know their own business very well, and that

when they make a mistake, it is mostly when some piece has been foisted on them, rather than accepted by them. No manager in his senses would exclude such a play as the 'Hunchback' from his theatre, or turn indifferently away from a proposal of Messrs. Taylor and Reade. Again, no sane manager will be caught by the mere literary pretensions of an author, or palm on the public a respectable poem, under the misconception that it will prove a popular drama. The grievance which authors endure from managerial prejudice, is, we suspect, of the very slenderest amount; and certainly, so far as we are acquainted with the "unacted drama," we are satisfied that its postponement to the Greek Calends is its only chance of escape from popular condemnation.

A modern pit, indeed, is no longer a bench of judicial criticism. That work is performed in a much more perfunctory style than it was formerly; and a new play seldom runs the gauntlet of scholars and artists assembled in the front rows. There was indeed much execrable criticism at a time when the drama was a popular amusement; the age itself was conventional, and admired a good deal, both in writing and acting, that would now be insufferably tedious. But far astray as our forefathers may have gone in the principles of good taste, they at least brought to the theatre an antecedent faith and earnestness from which we now shrink, or which are diverted to other and more permanent phases of art. Society is, in fact, in an adverse position to the drama, not so much because literature, on the one hand, partly usurps its domain, and partly anticipates its attractions, but also because it has reached a period of refinement incompatible with strong and natural emotions. We are become, in all that regards the theatre, a civil, similar, and impassive generation. To touch our emotions, we need not the imaginatively true, but the physically real. The visions which our ancestors saw with the mind's eye, must be embodied for us in palpable forms. If a king dies on the stage, he must suffer mortality's last pangs with all the circumstances of a death-bed; the expressive hints and bold outlines of our elder playwrights no longer suffice, we must see the patient writhe anatomically. We neither believe in part, nor prophesy in part; all must be made palpable to sight, no less than to feeling; and this lack of imagination in the spectators affects equally both those who enact and those who construct the scene.

POPULAR AMUSEMENTS.*

The subject of Popular Amusements, if we may trust to the evidence of book-catalogues, has hitherto been very imperfectly discussed. Of histories and treatises, indeed, classical or archæological, there is a sufficient supply; what is needed is examination of the question in all its bearings, from a social and ethical point of view. We desire to know, not so much the form of public recreations at different eras and among various nations, as the spirit which has actuated them, and the effect they have produced upon the character of mankind. We would have their physiognomy and philosophy more closely scrutinized, especially at the present moment, when the topic of public amusements seems likely to press itself on the attention of those who make and of those who obey the laws.

In the absence of any leading authority upon a question of no ordinary importance, we propose to interrogate the past briefly, and to ascertain, as far as our means of information and our limits allow, what

* Reprinted from the 'Westminster Review,' July 1856.

have been the expressions, among different nations, of their emotions earnest or mirthful; and what, socially or ethically, have been the results of popular amusements as delineated in the pages of history. We neither attempt nor presume to offer anything beyond the most general of surveys, and our object will be completely answered, if we succeed in drawing the attention of others to the records or the results of the spontaneous pastimes that often embody national character more completely than chronicles, state-papers, or even works of fiction.

We do not propose to enter again upon the Sabbath controversy, having so recently discussed it. This controversy indeed is rather a branch and corollary of the problem of public amusements than distinct and several in itself. If it be right and expedient to reflect whether recreations on one day in the week should be supplied or sanctioned, it is equally meet and right to consider whether it may not be advisable also to provide them for every reasonable interval of business. We have laws innumerable for making and keeping men grave; is it impossible to devise others which, if they do not make them merry, may at least elevate and refine them when disposed of their own accord to be so? Are Governments and statute-books, in short, to be always a terror to evil-doers, but never able or allowed to render the life of labour more endurable, or the life of leisure more dignified?

If an answer to these queries be sought in the

statute-books, or theological and ethical treatises,
during the last two centuries, it will not be favourable to the humanity of legislators or the wisdom of
divines. "Lex surda et inexorabilis est," says the
historian of Rome; and yet the Roman law was by
no means regardless of the recreations of the people.
And law is neither more deaf nor more inexorable
than divinity. Divines, not content with describing
this world as a world of probation, represent it as one
of durance also. To be happy, or to seem so, is to
tread the primrose path of sin. Philosophy taught
that health of mind was connected with, if not dependent upon, health of body; but theology, at least
such as is expounded from the pulpit or in books,
seldom if ever teaches anything of the sort: health
and cleanliness are sublunary considerations savour-
ing of the earth, and as for cheerfulness, it is not so
much as to be named in the congregation. Clearly,
then, as regards popular amusements, no hope is to
be looked for from the pulpit. Brave old Latimer indeed was of a different way of thinking, and delighted
in turning his hearers' attention to subjects connected
with their daily lives and recreations. But preachers
of his stamp are as rare as able-bodied and able-
minded bishops; and so far from desiring to send
home his hearers with renewed interest in their daily
life, the shepherd dismisses his flock with the assur-
ance that this is the worst possible of worlds, and
that the best use we can make of it is to be as un-

genial and uncomfortable in it as we can. Nor is the
flock generally a whit behind the shepherd in its relish
for discomfort.   The more vinegar and gall there
is in a sermon, the better it is relished; a cheerful
view of religion, or monitions to cater for body's
health as well as soul's health, would empty half the
churches in the United Kingdom.

Nor are legislators more disposed to look with an
eye of favour on public recreations than divines.
Littleton and Coke are as harsh and unsympathizing
as Calvin and Toplady.   "Legislators," says Sir
William Blackstone, "have for the most part chosen
to make the sanction of their laws rather *vindicatory*
than *remuneratory*, or to consist in punishments rather than in actual particular rewards.   Because, in
the first place, the quiet enjoyment and protection of
all our civil rights and liberties, which are the sure
and general consequence of obedience to the muni-
cipal law, are in themselves the best and most valuable of all rewards.   Because also, were the exercise of
every virtue to be enforced by the proposal of particular rewards, it were impossible for any State to
furnish stock enough for so profuse a bounty.   And
further, because the dread of evil is a much more
forcible principle of human action than the prospect
of good.   For which reasons, though a prudent bestowing of rewards is sometimes of exquisite use, yet
we find that those civil laws which enforce and enjoin
our duty, do seldom, if ever, propose any privilege or

gift to such as obey the law; but do constantly come armed with a penalty denounced against transgressors." We have no quarrel with this theory of rewards and punishments in its proper relations to the innocence or guilt of those who live under the law; yet the learned Justice of the Common Pleas has, in our opinion, by no means exhausted, and indeed has hardly touched on the philosophy of remuneration.

In whatever light we regard the State, whether as a parent regulating his children's actions, and exacting from them implicit obedience, or as a body of trustees appointed by the governed for their own good, it has a direct interest in the well-being of its members. It is not enough for them to be negatively benefited, as Blackstone insists, by the vigilance and wisdom of their rulers. Man is not formed to live by law alone, any more than he is by bread alone. His animal and intellectual faculties alike demand nurture and relaxation, and the Government which shuts its eyes to the amusements of the people, and considers that if life and goods be protected, all its duties are performed, beholds only half of its proper functions, and performs even that moiety imperfectly.

For, if work and its fair recompense be a preventive against crime, occasional leisure and recreation are not less good prophylactics in their way. The unbent mind is, at times, in as much peril from temptation as the unemployed. Even holidays are tedious, unless they interpose one kind of mental or bodily

activity for another: and the ale-house is filled as
much by those who are wearied with doing nothing,
as by the habitually intemperate. If proof of this
assertion be required, let the reader accompany us
for a moment, in imagination, to a village wake, or
even to the larger assembly of a town-fair. He will
see there an assemblage of people in better than their
ordinary attire, and bearing the traces of a recent
application of soap and water. The smith's sooty
visage looks scarified by his ablution, and the miller
and mason are no longer to be detected by their professional hue. If it be Whitsuntide or May-day,
there is some approach to a Feast of Tabernacles, for
the booths and skittle-grounds are decked with boughs
—the nearest approach now to pastoral sentiment in
England. But, if closely inspected, the whole affair
has a very business-like aspect. Listen to the conversation of the groups of holiday-makers, and it is
mostly of a serious cast—of markets and prices among
the men, of family casualties and scandal among the
women. Now and then, the children appear a little
exhilarated by the apparition of Mr. Merryman, or
the conversation of Mr. Punch. As the afternoon
wears on, it may be expected that the mirth will become fast and furious. The contrary is generally the
case. The men are besotted; the women are weary,
and anxious to return home: and, probably, in low
life as well as in high life, a day's pleasure is one of
the most truly wearisome in the year.

If we may trust to books, such matters were managed better in days of yore. Towns and villages were isolated from the capital, and from one another, by the badness or non-existence of roads : and the squire and lord of the manor was really a potentate in his own district, and, like other magnates, held his courts and levees. The fair was one of his annual ceremonies, and he or his family would no more have absented themselves from such gatherings, than from the family pew on Sundays. We cannot revert to the days of the Bracebridges and De Coverleys, but we may well doubt whether, if we have gained in wisdom, we have not lost something in social happiness. Certainly the isolation of classes from each other has increased with the facility of locomotion, and the wealthy now generally present themselves to their humbler neighbours under the grave aspect of founders of schools and restorers of churches, instead of partakers in their mirth and relaxations. He who shall devise a form of popular amusement attractive to every grade of society, will merit a civic wreath, as well as he who leads forth a colony, or opens new avenues to labour.

So many obstacles present themselves to this most desiderated discovery, that we have not the vanity even to suggest either an outline of it, or the direction in which it may, perhaps, be found. Our immediate object is, rather to survey briefly what has been the aspect of popular amusements in various nations,

thankfully accepted; the gold and the compliments
of the Egyptian Ptolemies were exceedingly welcome:
there was a time, they thought, for all things; a time
to refuse, and a time to receive favours; a time to
tread on the neck of kings, and a time to erect statues
to them in the Pnyx. And in the age of Menander
the latter of these seasons had arrived.

The revolutions in the public life of Athens affected
the character of its literary men. A century before
the birth of Menander its historians had been statesmen, its philosophers legislators, and its poets generals or magistrates. With the Sophists began the
separation of the lives practical and contemplative.
As regarded Athens, the Sophists were mostly aliens
by birth, who could exercise no function of the State;
and their gains as lecturers *de omni scibili* were increased by their independence of secular business, and
by their privilege of locomotion. Socrates, the most
practical of teachers, took his share bravely in all civil
and military duties; but on his disciple Plato the
mantle of the Sophists, in one respect, descended.
For the chief of the Academy was the first who
broached the questionable doctrine that it was the
duty of the philosopher to abstain from political employments; and the precepts of the master were carried
out by his scholar Aristotle, both in spirit and in
letter. The poets were not behindhand in claiming
the privilege of seclusion. Euripides, who, as we shall
see presently, approached the New Comedy in propor-

tion as he receded from the Elder Drama, was an author by profession; and in the age of Demosthenes, as we learn from the reiterated complaints of the orator himself, there was an increasing scarcity of men willing to devote their wealth and talents to the service of the State. When Menander began to write, the separation of the literary from the political world of Athens was nearly complete.

In Menander's generation, accordingly, we encounter a new phase of Athenian society,—a phase familiar enough in our own days, but unknown, or at least so unusual as to have escaped record, in the high and palmy days of the democracy. We then meet for the first time with the well-born and wealthy Athenian gentleman, whose public duties were fulfilled by the regular payment of his rates and taxes, by an occasional "turn-out" with the city militia, and an occasional attendance as juryman. Coarser or more ambitious spirits might wrangle in the public assembly, or covet diplomatic errands to Pella and Rhodes, or impair their patrimonies by equipping a troop of horse or a trireme. The utmost that a gentleman could be expected to do for his country's service was now and then to present one of its philosophical institutions with a talent or so, or to subscribe handsomely to a tragic chorus. Nor did his seclusion from public offices expose him to the charge of lukewarm patriotism. That virtue indeed had pretty nearly expired with Demosthenes; and there was little in the ex-

thrusting blunt javelins against their stately barges.
Professor Anderson might have met with his match
in Egypt, where the jugglers were as adroit as
the wizards; and no Neapolitan at the present day
plays the game of *mora* with more eagerness or livelier gesticulations than the Egyptians played at even-
and-odd. Dice are at least four thousand years old,
since they have been found, marked in the modern
manner, at Thebes; and draughts, coloured green and
yellow, and arranged in lines along a board, are represented at Benihassan. It would seem that the
two latter games were favourites with the Egyptian
clergy, owing doubtless to the tranquil and meditative turn of mind required for such pastimes. The
recreations of Thebes and Memphis did not, like the
Grecian panegyries, elevate or refine the taste of the
people; but neither do they imply either melancholy
or indolence in either exhibitors or spectators. If we
are to judge of their disposition by their sculptures,
we can hardly believe in the existence of a cheerful
Assyrian. Those aquiline countenances seem to defy
risus jocosque. We can imagine the Sphinx relaxing
into a smile, and even Memnon laughing on such
particular occasions as the Feast of Lamps, when all
Egypt was on the river, and as bousy as a piper.
There was indeed an essential difference in the lands
of Cham and Ninus. In the Nile valley, fringed on
each side by a desert, the population was close packed
in towns, and the wits of men were sharpened by

constant attrition with one another. Provision was
also plentiful; since the Egyptians generally were
vegetarians, and leguminous plants grew rapidly in
the teeming mud of Nilus. Neighbourhood and
abundance incline people to recreation, and even the
religious festivals of the calendar were antidotes to
sadness. Whereas the Assyrian was little more advanced in civilization than the pastoral races which
still occupy Upper Asia. Even his cities, although
notorious for license and the coarse ostentation of
wealth, reflected the image of a nomad encampment.
Vast parks were enclosed within the walls of Babylon,
and sheep and oxen grazed in multitudes in the heart
of Nineveh. Beyond their precincts, except in that
Mesopotamian district called the garden of Chaldæa,
enormous and arid plains stretched on every side,
and since vegetation extended but a little beyond the
banks of the Euphrates, population was scanty, and it
was often a day's journey from one village to another.
The character of the people corresponded to that of
their land. Both the Hebrew and Greek writers
agree in describing them as a fierce, grave, and violent race; with faces like an eagle's, with hair like
lions, terrible as archers, wasteful as locusts, and
more to be dreaded than the wolf or the hyena. Their
sculptures represent them as rending the lion and the
bear, and surrounded by the symbolisms of a race
conversant with the hardy life of shepherds—bronzed
by the morning frost and the noonday sun, tense in

L

fibre, eager of eye, with sinewy chests, and dilated nostrils, scenting the battle from afar. It is not among such a nation that we should seek for popular amusements. On the eastern verge of Asia, we come upon a people whom travellers have not unfrequently, although inaccurately, compared to the Egyptians. The Chinese resemble the inhabitants of the Nile valley only in the burdensome character of their ceremonies and in the sluggish permanence of their customs. It requires an effort of the imagination to picture to ourselves a youthful or a cheerful Chinese. From his cradle and swaddling-clothes, he is the slave of prescription. The spontaneous impulses of his childhood are repressed by education, and the recreations of his manhood are grave, solemn, and ungenial. No feeling of the beautiful is apparent in any of his pursuits or productions; he paints, designs, and carves as his forefathers did centuries ago; his demeanour and ordinary speech are regulated by strict laws; and what is not written in the books of the wise, is not permitted to be done or said without a serious breach of law and decorum. There is indeed a certain impressive grandeur in many of his festivals, in his prayers at the tomb of his ancestors, his ever-burning lamps, and his reverence for what his teachers have prescribed or time has hallowed. But China is not the land of cheerfulness: even its amusements bear a weighty and a serious brow; and the land presents the aspect which the Greeks attributed to their Hades

—a land where all things always seem the same, and where the sports and exercises of youth afford no pleasure and admit of no variety. Throughout Asia, indeed, an air of melancholy prevails which is not wholly attributable to the civil or spiritual despotism of its rulers and its castes. Man in those regions is a weed; he is dwarfed by the colossal scale on which nature works: his religions are ancient, monumental, elaborate, and cruel; his philosophy is ascetic and contemplative; and his relaxations partake of the earnest and sombre genius of his creeds, traditions, and institutions.

It is from the inventive and practical sons of Hellas that we must seek for the true theory and example of popular amusements. The Greeks were the first to announce the law of education—that it should consist in nearly equal proportion of the arts which elevate the mind and the exercises which strengthen the body. The combination of the *musical* with the *gymnastic* was first displayed in the public games of Greece, and was repeated in the daily life of every Grecian commonwealth. So salient a feature was this of Hellenic manners, that we find Paul of Tarsus drawing from the race-course one of his liveliest and most expressive illustrations, and Plato preluding so many of his dialogues with references to the palæstra, the stadium, and the sports that accompanied the festivals of Pallas, Apollo, and Ceres. "All pastimes," says Roger Ascham, "generally, which

be joyned with labour and in open place, and on the
day-lightc, be not only comelic and decent, but verie
necessaric for a courtly gentleman;" and the Greeks,
although they admitted a certain coarseness of speech
and action, which the greater decency or the better
regulated hypocrisy of modern life prohibits, were, in
comparison with other contemporary nations, a race
of "courtly gentlemen." It was deemed discreditable
for any one above the condition of a slave or a bar-
barian, to be unable to express himself in society or
in public with freedom and case upon any topic of
discussion: he was deemed awkward and ill-trained
who could not add to the conviviality of the table by
song or recitation; and it needed all the fame and
ingenuity of Themistocles to excuse himself for his
inability to play on the flute.   It was considered un-
beseeming a citizen to be inexpert in any warlike or
manly accomplishment, and the Greek admiration for
physical beauty rendered indispensable the exercises
that develope the muscles or give precision to the
eye and the hand.   The instincts of the people were
nurtured by the habits of their daily life.   It was for
women to be sedentary, because, according to the
erroneous notions of her master, she was a slave.
But an indolent or invalid man was a prodigy and a
laughing-stock; and some of Plato's keenest satire is
pointed against the self-indulgence of the Sophists
who sat by the stove and lapped themselves in cloaks
and blankets.   The ceremonials of the Christian

Church have, in all ages, commanded the applause of the artist and attracted the admiration of the vulgar. But the most gorgeous festivals of the Roman and Byzantine priesthood are ignoble beside the Olympic Games or the Greek Panegyrics of Athens and Delos. In the one, the symbolisms of religion affect the faith or imagination only of the spectators, who gaze, a profane herd, upon the drama of the sanctuary, but are not permitted to take part in the performance. The worship of the Greeks was of a more catholic and ennobling kind. No free man was excluded from the contests of the arena: the cost of the chariot race, indeed, restricted its full enjoyment to the wealthy, but, at least in the earlier and better days, the manly exercises of the Pentathlon were open to the young, the vigorous, and the handsome. Godlike and heroic men were esteemed the best exponents of the bounty and providence of the gods; and Apollo was venerated not only as the giver of light and health, but also as the model of manly strength and grace. It was a decline both in art and in national feeling, when the boxers and wrestlers became merely professional artists, trained and dieted like our tumblers and prize-fighters to feats of agility and strength, and sacrificing the music, *i. e.* the intellectual portion of their abilities, to the gymnastic or physical. The Crotoniate Milo, whose stalwart arms could rive an oak, or whose brawny shoulders could carry off an ox, was deeply versed in the science of Pythagoras, and was applauded by the spectators as the mortal representative of the beautiful sons of Leda. The religion of the Greeks carefully watched over three principal objects of petition in the prayers of our church; nor was its care limited to verbal petition, nor were the worshipers contented with periodical acknowledgment that the well-being of man consists in a judicious regulation of "mind, body, and estate." The *mind* was cared for by the combination of intellectual with gymnastic exhibitions; and the audience at Elis or Corinth expected with as much eagerness the song in honour of the conqueror, as the feats which obtained for him the laurel or parsley coronal. The *body* was regarded as well by the exercises which fostered its vigour, grace, and suppleness, as by the temperance in all things which whosoever contended for the prize must observe. And the *estate* was also an object of solicitude, since temperance and hardihood are incompatible with luxury and sloth. We may affect to smile or sigh at the shallowness or incongruity of the creed of Greece, but we must often blush, amid the comparative effeminacy of modern manners, at the manlier practice of the worshipers of Zeus and Athéné. It is needless to expatiate on the artistic genius of the Greeks further than to note its intimate connection with the physical character of the people. The town of Sicyon was probably not more extensive than the least of the provincial capitals of England, yet it contained, if we may credit Pausanias,

more masterpieces of art than at this moment can be
found in all London. The models of the artist were
not far to seek. The streets, the market-place, and
the gymnasium afforded them; and the long conservation of physical beauty which survived the extinction
of freedom, is to be ascribed to the passion of the
Greeks for gymnastic discipline. The traces of this
passion are visible in the latest ages of Hellenic literature. Lucian, Plutarch, and Dion Chrysostom
dwell on the vigour and beauty of the race in their
time, and generally couple their commendations of natural graces with allusions to the training schools or
the public games. The noblest of the Greek writers,
indeed, deplore the comparative decline of their countrymen in physical qualities, and ascribe the inferiority of their contemporaries to departure from the
hardy habits of their forefathers. Aristophanes contrasts the curled darlings of his time with the big,
brawny men who fought with the Persians at Salamis
and Platæa; and Demosthenes taunts his hearers with
their reluctance to serve their country in the fleet or
the phalanx. The ancient spirit however did not wholly
die, until the Hellenic race itself expired under the
lazy and oppressive despotism of the Byzantine Cæsars.
The games of the hippodrome were no substitute
for the periodical festivals at Elis and the Isthmus.
The charioteers of the *green* and *blue* factions were
hirelings; the body-guards of Justinian and Alexius
were recruited in Britain and the Rhine-land, and

the flower of Grecian life drooped and dwindled in the unwholesome atmosphere of the Bar and the Church.

In the national amusements of the Greeks the gymnastic element preponderated, and the proportion is just, since it is not desirable that many men should devote themselves to literature, while it imports the general good that every member of the community should, unless physically disabled, be active, healthy, and brave. For the musical or intellectual element, the Greeks thought that they had provided abundantly by the Dionysiac festivals; and assuredly the Drama has never assumed a more august and imposing form than it presented yearly at Athens. We are not insensible to the ampler and nobler dimensions of the Romantic Drama as compared with the Classical, nor disinclined to admit that in Shakespeare's and Calderon's plays a more profoundly religious, or rather a more profoundly humane, element exists than is to be found in the Orestcia or the Antigone. Viewed however in the light of popular amusements, the palm must be awarded to the Greek Drama. The scrupulousness or superstition of the Church has unfortunately divorced the Theatre from the ritual or the dogmas of religion; or when they have occasionally entered into co-partnership, as in the instances of Calderon's 'Autos' and Racine's scriptural tragedies, the union has been brief, and unfavourable to the more popular objects of the Drama. The hostility of the Church to the Theatre

commenced with the just repugnance of all wise and
good men to the atrocities of the Roman stage. The
coarseness and license in which Aristophanes occasionally indulges would have appeared faint and feeble
to a Roman inured to the representations at the Me-
galesian and Floral Games; and if the libels of Pro-
copius contain any admixture of truth, the impurities of Rome were far surpassed by those of Constantinople. The antagonism of the Church to the Theatre was accordingly just in its origin, but it has been
prejudicial equally to dramatic art and to popular recreation. At the Dionysiac festivals of Greece they
went hand in hand,—art was ennobled, recreation
acquired an ethical importance, and the creed of
the people was presented under the attractive forms
of solemn and purifying emotions. In the fables of
Œdipus, Electra, and Antigone, the presence of a
spiritual power, righting the secret wrongs, appalling
the guilty, and justifying the innocent, was made
manifest, nor could any attentive and thoughtful
spectator depart from the representation of Prometheus without a conviction that the sacrifice of suffering is not less acceptable to the gods than the sacrifice of action. The Attic Drama was indeed the
most superb and solemn liturgy of the Hellenic religion. The Greeks thus realized in their practice
nearly every condition involved in the theory of
popular amusements. They provided for the intellectual and physical improvement of the people both

locally and nationally. Their great panegyrics were common to all who were not barbarians,—*i. e.* to all who traced their ancestry from Pelops, Ion, and the Heracleids, or who, though of foreign extraction, were admitted—a rare privilege—for some signal service into the family of Hellas; and their local institutions catered for the health, instruction, and cheerfulness of the several communities. The civilization of Christendom has, in some respects, advanced beyond that of the Hellenic race. It has improved, though it is still very far from apprehending, the proper relations and position of women; it has generally abolished slavery, although the change from myriads of slaves to myriads of paupers is a brief step only in the right direction, and is at lamentable variance with the doctrines of a religion professing to regard all men as brethren, and wealth as dross. It has established munificent public charities, which were known in a rude form only to antiquity, and embraced freemen alone; and if it has not extirpated, it has ceased to countenance openly such anomalous vices as disgraced even the best ages of Greece and Rome. But the parallel must here break off. No Christian state has hitherto devised or effected a system of public education worthy to be put in the scale with that of Greece. We have yet much to learn from both the Dorian and Ionian races in the art of rendering the masses intelligent, healthy, and alert.

The virtues of the Romans, which elicited the applause of the most ethical of historians, were civil and political rather than intellectual. Polybius, who had beheld the arts and refinements of Greece unimpaired by conquest and unvitiated by neglect, preferred to them the hardy Roman qualities of legislation and government. The most accomplished of the Latin poets agreed with the grave historian in this estimate of his countrymen, and bade them leave to others the sculptor's and the painter's art, and devote themselves to law, administration, and agriculture. In whatsoever related to art and education, indeed, Rome, as compared with Greece, or even Etruria, was rude and uninventive, and even on its colossal roads and aqueducts is impressed the stamp of material energy more than of grace or contrivance. The popular amusements of Rome reflected the practical genius of its people. They were symbolic of war and agriculture. The games of the Circus mimicked the strife of the battle-field; and the vernal and autumnal festivals represented by their altars of sod and their garlands of flowers the simple thanksgivings of the tillers of the soil. Even from the earliest times an ethical, and not an artistic spirit, is visible in their recreations, and in their seasons of relaxation they indulged in mementos of the precariousness of life. Of all Roman exhibitions, the Secular Games were, both from their occasion and their ceremonial, the most suggestive of sad and sober thoughts. They were

celebrated, in compliance with a cyclical computation
of the Etruscans, once only in a hundred or a hundred
and ten years; the ambition or policy of the Cæsars,
indeed, sometimes abridged the regular term; but
even a jubilee occurring once only in fifty years, is
well adapted to inspire the spectators with solemn
reflections. The usual interval, however, between the
Secular Games exceeded the ordinary term of life; and
as none of the spectators had already seen them, none
could flatter themselves with the hope of beholding
them again. The sacrifices were performed during
three nights on the banks of the Tiber; the darkness
was dispelled by innumerable lamps and torches, and
the proper silence of the hour was broken by music
and dancing. Heralds, some days before the solemnity commenced, invited the citizens to a spectacle
which no one had ever beheld, and none would behold again. The fruits of the earth were offered to
the Destinies, and a chorus of twenty-seven youths
and as many virgins of noble families, whose parents
were both alive, implored, in appropriate hymns, the
gods in favour of the present and of the rising generation. A more striking contrast can hardly be conceived than that which this grave religious spectacle
presents to the daylight cheerfulness and redun-
dant life of an Olympic Festival. It was difficult,
indeed, to make the senate or people of Rome laugh
at anything short of buffoonery; or to rouse their
emotions by anything except blows and bloodshed.

They would hurry out of the theatre from the woes of Atreus or the delicate wit of the Adelphi, on the first call of the "elephants" or "rope-dancers" in the streets; and Ennius then, like Shakespeare now, was unpalatable to the benches, unless armies swept across the stage, and the wardrobe blazed with purple and gold. And hitherto we have noticed the least noxious of Roman spectacles. It was a virtuous age when a few elephants driven by slaves across the arena contented the people; it was a moderate one when a few pairs of gladiators sufficed for the consular or prætorian games. Lord Bacon has pronounced that—"the triumph amongst the Romans was not pageants or gaudery, but one of the wisest and noblest institutions that ever was; for it contained three things—honour to the general, riches to the treasury out of the spoils, and donatives to the army." The triumph however, with all deference to so high an authority, we believe to have been one of the effective causes in producing that hardness of heart which marked all the dealings of Rome with the conquered and the slave. It inured the people to regard with callousness or exultation private suffering and public mutations. Kings bound in chains and nobles in links of iron, and afterwards doomed to a swift or lingering death in the Mamertine dungeon or the solitary *ergastulum*, were spectacles engendering pride and cruelty, and affording no compensation by their ethical or artistic suggestions.

The corollary of the triumph was the combat of wild beasts and gladiators. Both the brute and the human nature were the captives of the bow and spear; and the victor conceived that he had gained the right to torture and destroy either of them for his own good pleasure. In the last century of the Commonwealth, and under all the worse emperors, the popular amusements of the Romans may be summed up under the two heads of cruelty and licentiousness. At the more cheerful spectacles no modest woman could be present, although few Roman matrons and maidens were absent from them; from the graver spectacles no one could depart without sickness of heart, or with hearts deadened and indurated, and lapsed below all depths of pity or terror.

The drama can hardly be reckoned among the popular amusements of the Romans. National subjects for theatrical representation, they had none; party politics were too acrimonious among them for the stories of Coriolanus or Manlius to be safe or attractive. The deeds of the house of Tarquin, however well suited to the tragic muse, reminded them at once of their superstitious hatred of the kingly name and of the humble origin of the Commonwealth. The formality of domestic life and manners left hardly any scope or margin for comedy, and grave senators ill-brooked jests and intrigues at the expense of their haughty Portias and Æmilias. Their comedy was accordingly a servile copy of the later comedy of the

Greeks, both in its plots, manners, and *dramatis personæ*. But of Greek manners, the Roman populace knew about as much as Rotherhithe knows of Belgravia; and the refined wit of Terence was as unintelligible to Caius of the Suburra, as the 'School for Scandal' would be to the frequenters of the Victoria Theatre. We need not expatiate on an amusement which, being patronized only in the saloons of the Scipios, has no claim to the adjunct "popular." The Italians, however, though their dramatic literature has in all periods been about the most scantily appointed in Europe, were nevertheless a highly dramatic race. Their quick emotions express themselves in ready and ingenious pantomime, and the native farce was the lineal ancestor of the burlesques which, from the Alps to the extremity of the peninsula, are still a source of the keenest enjoyment to the vulgar. Latin literature has sustained no heavier loss than that of the 'Fabulæ Atellanæ.' They were of a higher order than the mimes or farces; were regular compositions, divided into five acts, marked by refined humour, and acted by free-born citizens. Had a single specimen of these native comedies been preserved, we might perhaps have rated Roman comedy higher. But equally as respected its political development and its popular recreations, it was the misfortune of the Romans to be crushed and corrupted by the weight and rapidity of their conquests. A martial and agricultural race, hardy, coarse, and uncivilized, was suddenly enriched by the treasures of Greece, Asia, and Gaul. License and enjoyment immediately succeeded to frugal severity of life; and the Romans, too impatient to cultivate their native arts, purchased wholesale the ready-made stock of the more advanced and ingenious Greeks. Noise, glare, and prodigal expenditure were at once the bane of the Roman theatre and its literature. Poets and actors cannot always be found; but the artificer and the upholsterer are always to be hired, and in the pantomime they found ample room for their costly and eccentric devices. A numerous and idle population, for whom the theatre was provided *gratis*, demanded houses too spacious for the human voice, or by their rude clamours drowned the recitation of the actors. But the pantomime, appealing to the eye alone, and admitting of sumptuous decoration, entranced thousands of spectators, and the most popular of Roman dramatic entertainments dispensed with the playwright altogether. Of the three favourite public recreations of the Romans, the Triumph, the Spectacles, and the Theatre, not one promoted the refinement of the people, or tended to the encouragement of the artist. The passion for boxers, fencers, and wild beasts survived the Republic and exhausted the treasures of the Empire. The most politic and virtuous of the Cæsars repressed the fury of the people for such exhibitions; but the example of Trajan and the Antonines was disregarded by Commodus and Caracalla, and when the capital of the Empire was transplanted to the shores of the Bosphorus, the enormities of the pantomime and the race-course migrated also from the Colosseum to the Hippodrome.

That we may not be supposed to have exaggerated the scale of the public amusements of Rome, or their demoralizing effects on the spectators, we add the following brief sketches of three remarkable spectacles at eras very distant from one another,—two of which were exhibited in the Plain of Mars, at Rome, and the third in the Circus at Constantinople.

1. In the 700th year of the City, the popularity of Cneius Pompeius was on the wane, and he laboured to revive it by the magnificence of his exhibitions. Hitherto the Roman theatres had been built of wood, and were removed after the spectacles had terminated. Now a theatre was constructed of stone, and designed for permanence. Forty thousand persons, no small portion of the resident population of the city, were accommodated within its walls; and it was decorated with such a profusion of gold, marble, and gems, as had never yet been witnessed out of Alexandria or Babylon, when "Egypt with Assyria strove in luxury." The consecration of this theatre, which, as a pretext for its permanence, was dedicated to Venus Victrix, was celebrated with music, chariot races, and all the games of the palæstra. During five successive days, five hundred lions were hunted and slaughtered in the arena. Eighteen elephants

were made to fight with trained bands of gladiators;
and the cries and agonies of these noble and sagacious animals inspired even the brutalized crowd with
pity and disgust. Stage plays were combined with
these grosser spectacles; but the verses of Pacuvius
and Ennius were imperfectly heard amid the din and
tumult of such an assembly, and the games broke up
amid general murmurs at the inefficiency of the display, and the exhibitor's bad taste.

2. Three centuries had elapsed, and the extravagances of the arena had kept pace with the corruption of the times and the prodigality of the Cæsars,
when Carinus surpassed all his predecessors by the
pomp with which he celebrated the Roman games.
They had been established by the founder of the city,
and, with few interruptions, were exhibited annually
during a period of nearly one thousand years. On
this occasion they were displayed in the amphitheatre
of Titus, which has obtained and so well deserves the
epithet of Colossal. Into the huge ellipse of this
vast conclave, sixty-four *vomitories* poured forth an
immense multitude, without trouble or confusion.
The slopes of the interior were filled and surrounded
by sixty or eighty rows of marble seats, covered with
cushions, and capable of containing above fourscore
thousand spectators. The senatorial, equestrian, and
plebeian orders—these empty distinctions were retained even under the equality of despotism—each
occupied its peculiar station; and in the centre, a

golden canopy, and the glittering cuirasses of the
body-guard, marked out the imperial box. The
spectators were protected from the sun and rain by
purple awnings, occasionally drawn over their heads.
Fountains cooled and aromatics impregnated the air
with grateful odours; and the stage itself was strewn
with parti-coloured sand, arranged in devices, like
the pattern of a carpet. The scenery and mechanism
of the Drama corresponded to the luxury of the theatre. The stage itself was shifted according to the
exigencies of the performance. At one moment, it
presented a vast lake covered with armed vessels, and
replenished with the monsters of the deep; at another,
the spectators beheld the garden of the Hesperides, or
the rocks and caverns of Thrace. The appointments
of the Circus were not less sumptuous. The wild
beasts were surrounded by a sylvan scene. A forest
of large trees, torn up by the roots, was transplanted
into the midst of the arena. This umbrageous space
was immediately filled with a thousand ostriches, a
thousand stags, a thousand fallow-deer, and a thousand wild-boars, all of which were indiscriminately
slaughtered before evening. On the following day, a
hundred lions, a hundred lionesses, two hundred
leopards, and three hundred wild boars, were massa-
cred; and, amid such profusion, we may credit the
statement of a contemporary poet, that the nets designed as a defence against the wild beasts were of
gold wire, that the porticoes were gilded, and the

balustrades which divided the rows of spectators, studded with a mosaic of precious stones. It is needless to comment upon the splendour and barbarism of such popular amusements.

3. But these were trivial and even harmless follies compared with the factions and frenzy of the Byzantine hippodrome. It is not easy to decide whether the capital of the Eastern Empire suffered more from the feuds of the Church or of the Circus. The election of a bishop or a patriarch was not seldom accompanied with bloodshed; and the factions of the charioteers on more than one occasion suspended the actions of Government, and shook the imperial throne. The lively fancy of the Greeks, so alert in splitting hairs in the sublimest mysteries of religion, was equally active in ascribing symbolic meanings to the colours worn on the race-course. The *white* was supposed to be typical of the snows of winter, the *red* of the summer dog-star, the *green* of the verdure of spring, and the *blue* or *azure* of the mingled tints of autumn. Omens were drawn from their respective victories; and the bettors on a favourite colour conceived that on the issue of their wager depended, not only money and estates, but also a plentiful harvest or a prosperous navigation. Twenty-five *heats* were run in the same day; and, as each faction furnished one chariot for every course, one hundred chariots in the same day started for the goal. It would have been happy for the State, if the contests had been

limited to the Circus. But political passions were infused into popular amusement, and the greens and blues alternately enjoyed and abused the pleasures of victory. Families were split into opposite factions; quarters of the city were distracted by irreconcileable feuds; the Cæsars themselves took part with one or the other livery; and lust, rapine, and murder ranged, unreproved and unchecked, under the sway of favourite charioteers. Their occasional union was even more fatal to public order than their ordinary division; and, at one crisis of these Saturnalia, the royal galleys were moored at the garden gate of the Blachernal palace, ready to convey the trembling Emperor and his household to some safe and distant retreat. From the capital, this pestilence was diffused into the provinces and cities of the East: Antioch and Alexandria were torn by the factions of the racecourse: and the excesses and extravagances of an idle and useless recreation that wasted the strength and treasures of the Empire, may fairly be enumerated among the causes of its decrepitude and decline.

Whatever may have been the doctrinal influence of Christianity upon the vices and follies of a superannuated fabric of society, its higher and more severe morality cannot be questioned. Even the selfish interests of mankind were enlisted in favour of a creed which promoted the household virtues and family union, and restrained crimes of such flagrant dye as convulsed the later days of the Pagan world. The fathers of the Church have often been censured for the intolerant zeal of their attacks on art and the theatre; but to understand and excuse them, it is only necessary for us to contemplate what dramatic exhibitions had become. Even the foregoing sketches of the license of the Roman amphitheatre and the Byzantine race-course will suffice to justify Chrysostom or Tertullian's indignation at the spectacles, and to accept even the aid of bigotry against a moral pestilence so deeply rooted and so widely diffused. The strong virtues of the barbarians in time seconded the reclamations of the Church; and, although the amusements of Christendom are not unstained by cruelty and license, they have never, in the worst epochs, approached the excesses of either capital of the Roman Empire.

Our route would be too devious were we to trace the various popular amusements of Europe, after it was broken up into communities, each displaying its several character. We must content ourselves with arranging, under a few distinct heads, the recreations which expressed the pleasures or the passions of the people. For centuries after its emancipation from the yoke of Rome, the normal condition of Europe was one of war and isolation. There was little intercourse between its kingdoms; there were few diplomatic transactions between its crowns; the sea was insecure; the great roads which Rome had drawn from every province of its empire to the Milliarium in the forum were neglected or broken up; and each petty state was at leisure to mature and develope its own institutions and amusements. Between the cities and the country a marked distinction had grown up. The recreations of the nobles were the chase and the tournament: those of the citizens, the processions and symbolisms of the guilds. The one naturally displayed the image of war : the other exhibited the works and benefits of industry and peace. As an example of these general characteristics, we will dwell for an instant upon the opposite amusements of the Spaniards and the Flemings, as respectively the exponents of nations great in arms and thrifty and splendid in peace.

The Spaniards were in many of their predilections genuine descendants of Rome. They hated commerce, and willingly resigned retail and mechanical trades into the hands of Moriscos, Germans, or French, or any strangers who had settled among them—much as the Romans left their shops and warehouses to Greek or Syrian freedmen and slaves. The love of idleness was accompanied with a passion for amusement, and the recreations of the Spaniards were fierce, sombre, and gorgeous in their character. For the splendour of their tournaments, we need only refer to their ballad literature; for the savage license of the bull-fight, to every book of travels in the Peninsula; and for the sumptuousness of their theatrical decorations, to the records of their Drama, and even the stage directions of their plays. It was in vain for the Cortes to express, as they did as early as 1555, their disapprobation of the bull-fights. The zest for them was too deeply seated in the temper of the people. It was useless for the treasurers of the royal household to remonstrate against the profusion of the Theatre Royal; the nobles demanded and the king sanctioned the outlay. With the attachment to habit and the aversion from change that still mark the Spanish people, the tournament lingered among them long after it became an empty and unmeaning spectacle in the rest of Europe. "The Spaniard of 1840," writes George Borrow, "is the Spaniard of four centuries ago;" he still delights to charge the bull with his lance, and drive him down the narrow mountain track to the river; he is a tamer of horses; a believer in wizards; a sworn foe to Jews and Moors, and labour; his repose cannot be too profound, his paroxysms of recreation and enjoyment too fervid or fierce.

His Flemish and Dutch subjects presented equally in their occupations and amusements the most complete contrast to the Spaniard. The wealthy and comfortable burghers of Antwerp, Ghent, Bruges, and Leyden, had small delight in war or the chase, in torturing beasts, or in the savour of roasted heretics. Their delight was to see, on occasions of ceremony or rejoicing, oxen roasted whole in the market-place, wine gushing from the pipes of the fountains, men climbing high poles, and women running races for prizes, and festive lanterns burning at night on the belfries of their cities. The rhetorical guilds of the Flemings were also in marked contrast to the dramatic entertainments of the Spaniards. The fancy of the poet and the stores of classic or romantic story were ransacked for the uses of the theatres of Madrid and Seville; and, with the exception of moveable scenery, they lacked little of the pomp and splendour of Parisian or London playhouses. The imagination of the Netherlanders was more easily contented, or of a more practical kind. Their spectacles embodied, in sensible imagery, wise saws and pregnant maxims, and symbolized the household and commercial virtues that render their possessors easy in person and in circumstances. A high day at Madrid in the reign of Philip IV. was in all essential respects the image of a high day in the reign of Ferdinand and Isabella. The nobles, mounted on Arabian barbs, carried an estate on their backs invested in silks, gems, and costly armour, and paraded their finery before the dark eyes hardly concealed by the lattices or veils which the semi-oriental jealousy of Spanish fathers, brothers, and husbands devised and demanded. The Flemings visited one another on gala-days, dressed in cumbrous velvets and stiff brocades, and were solemnly drawn in antique and richly adorned coaches, displaying on their panels the strangest allegorical

M

emblems of peace, plenty, and thrift. The fortunes and character of the nations were reflected in these their popular amusements. The Netherlanders grew and remained rich; the Spaniards became, and have remained poor unto this day. The mines of the Indies poured their wealth eventually into the laps of the Flemings and the Hollanders; since Antwerp and Rotterdam supplied Seville and Barcelona with the wares which the Spaniard deemed it beneath his dignity to manufacture, or even to vend when imported. "More business," says a shrewd Venetian envoy, "is done in Antwerp in a month than at Cadiz or Barcelona in two years."

We must afford space for one more glimpse at the recreations of Southern Europe before turning to the popular amusements of our own land. Florence, we are told by the chroniclers, Malaspini and Villani, was, towards the end of the thirteenth century, eminently prosperous and happy. The city abounded in mirth and festivity: jugglers, buffoons, and mountebanks poured in from all the Italian states to share the bounty of its princely merchants, who, although generally plain and frugal in their private life and households, were sumptuous and hospitable in their public entertainments. Easter was an especial season for revelry. The wealthier Florentines then kept open house, and welcomed multitudes of poets, musicians, dancers, jesters, players, and charlatans of every sort, and none of those who pleased in order to live were permitted to depart without considerable *largesse*, whether in the form of money, or of rich dresses and ornaments.

In the sonnets of Folgore da San Gimignano, a poet of the year 1260, we obtain an insight into the amusements of the gentlemen of Siena at that period. The bard follows the approved almanac-fashion in prescribing to his readers what they are to eat, drink, and avoid, and how to disport themselves in each month in order to cause their days to pass pleasantly. We select a few instances of his comfortable counsels.

In January he bids his friends to keep large fires in well-lit rooms; to have their bed-chambers splendidly furnished with silken sheets and fur coverlets. The servants must be snugly clad in woollens and cloth of Douay; and there should be plenty of confectionery. Out-of-doors, the gentlemen are to amuse themselves by throwing soft snow-balls at the young ladies whom they may happen to meet in their walks. When tired with these exertions, they must take a good allowance of repose.

This *dolce far niente* however is not to endure for ever. Even the existence of a Sybarite, if persevered in too long, will grow tedious. So in February these pleasant gentlemen must rise betimes and "hunt the deer," the wild goat and boar, "with hound and horn." At night they shall come merrily home to excellent wine, a smoking kitchen, and a song.

In March, when the sun rides high in Aries, and

strong exercise is not so needful to warm the blood,
fishing is to be substituted for hunting; they are now
to migrate from their town-houses to their suburban
villas and palaces, and to procure every delight that
will make time run smoothly; but without monk or
priest. "Let those crazy shavelings," says the irre-
verent poet, "go and preach, for they abound in lies."
The Italians appear to have known nothing of Parson
Supple, who could ride nearly as well and drink quite
as well as Squire Western himself.

In April the scene changes to an Arcadian life,
amid flowery fields, fountains, and lawns; and the
general prescription is—mules, palfreys, and steeds
from Spain, songs and dances from Provence, and
new instruments of music fresh from Germany.
There is, indeed, much national physiognomy involved in these maxims. Monks are excluded from
this paradise, but not Eves; for dames and damsels
saunter along with these gay Sienese bachelors,
through groves and gardens where all would honour
them, and bend their knee before the queen, the lady
of beauty, to whom the poet offers a crown of jewels,
even of the finest jewels of Prester John, King of
Babylonia.

May brought with it troops of light well-trained
horses, springy, spirited, and swift, with head and
breast well armed; and tinkling bells and banners,
and rich trappings; many-coloured mantles, light
round shields and polished weapons, which were not

to be borne in vain, for there must be breaking of spears and shock of lances; and the reward of chivalry shall be flowers of every hue, showers of garlands from balcony and casement, and flights of golden oranges tossed up in turn; and youths and maidens kissing mouth and cheek, and discoursing of happiness and love.

We have not space to follow this joyous calendar through the rolling year, and recommend such of our readers as may have been led to envy life at Siena, to procure the poems of Messer San Gimignano. The counsels for October however are too extraordinary to be passed over. The poet seems to have thought, with the adage, that—

> " He who drinks and goes to bed sober,
> Falls as the leaves do, and dies in October."

For then, he says, it is good to visit a house where a good stud is kept, to follow sports on foot or horseback, dance at night, drink good wine and get tipsy; "as in good sooth there is no better life." And after the morning's ablutions, wine and roast meat are once more an excellent medicine, for they will give good spirits, and preserve them in better health than that of fishes in lake, river, or sea, "because thus they would be leading a more Christian life !"

An unlucky wag of the time, Cene della Citarra of Arezzo, parodied these sonnets of Messer Folgore's, and imparted his notions of the enjoyments of the poor. We regret our inability to look on this picture also, since the two would enable ùs to present a tolerably complete outline of the popular amusements of Italy.

It is much to be regretted that those who have written on symbolisms, have for the most part viewed the subject from merely a theological point of view, or at least have restricted their researches to the bare demands of archæology.   The subject of popular amusements would derive much light from a history of the symbols adopted by various nations, and especially from those belonging to the trading corporations and guilds.   We can afford however to hint only at an unworked vein of inquiry that would probably illustrate better than the history of cabinets and campaigns the social development and peculiarities of a people.   The guilds of Europe, with their banners, devices, and periodical festivals, date from a remote antiquity, and although they were considerably modified by Christian emblems and ideas, they lurk in many an obscure corner of Roman and oriental record.

The gravity with which we Englishmen disport ourselves, appeared to Froissart, accustomed to the lighter and more graceful mirth of France, a feature of peculiar significance in the national character.   It is indeed impossible to deny that the English have a relish for broad fun, since have we not Fielding's, and Smollett's, and Dickens's novels, and Shakespeare's Falstaff, constables, and clowns?   But we

are not a demonstrative people like the Athenians
and the French, and although our comedy is as rich
as that of Aristophanes and Molière, our assemblies
and recreations have assuredly an air of steady and
serious business. We would not indeed exchange
the general sobriety of our cities for the indiscriminate levity of Vienna, nor are we disposed to regard
it as a symptom of any constitutional or deep-seated
melancholy. We ascribe it rather to the more domestic character of our habits, as compared with
those of most Continental nations. Even sadness can
seldom maintain its equable demeanour in a crowd,
where the attention is perpetually diverted from self
by the passing objects, the converse and gesticulations going on on every side. The liveliest people of
antiquity were the Athenians, whose life was almost
passed in the streets; external air, and restlessness,
are provocatives, if not to mirth, at least to com-
panionship; and a population that has scarcely a
home, is generally to outward semblance noisy and
demonstrative. If physiognomy indeed be an index
of the cheerfulness or the gravity of a people, we are
inclined to think that an English crowd will bear
comparison with that of any country for a general
expression of content. More anxious faces will be
met with in Paris or New York in an hour than
London exhibits in a week; although indeed on the
occasion of a spectacle or a general holiday, there will
be in both the former cities greater noise and osten-

tation of pleasure. We seldom scream, shout, or give
way to inextinguishable laughter; but neither do we
so often shed tears, rend our hair, or commit suicide.
If we possess no sober certainty of waking bliss as
a nation, and exercise to the full our privilege of
grumbling at the weather, the crops, and the Government, we have fewer *émeutes*, fewer revolutions, fewer
breakings-up of the great central abysses of passion,
than have occurred among nations claiming to be
livelier and more sensitive than ourselves. But our
immediate business is with the national character as
exhibited or suggested in its seasons of relaxation;
and it must be admitted that these for the most part
are of a saturnine complexion. A manly vigour from
the earliest times is perceptible in the recreations of
the English nation. After the first pressure of the
Norman yoke was lightened, and the conquerors had
ceased to regard the conquered with scornful or jealous eyes, the native sports of the Saxons were permitted them and even encouraged. The earlier wars
of the Norman kings with France had been waged
chiefly with the lances and battle-axes of their own
retainers; but the efficiency of the English archers
manifested itself so strikingly on many critical occasions, that the practice of the bow was diligently enforced by the Plantagenets. Nor after the close of
the Barons' wars did the Tudors overlook this formidable adjunct to the rude artillery of their day; and
indeed throughout the fifteenth century, nothing more

surely proves the good understanding between the
Government and the people than the universal practice of bearing arms. Every man was a soldier, and
equipped according to his rank and means with corresponding armour and weapons. The exercises of
the tilt-yard at the Hall or Castle were reserved for
those of gentle birth; and the imitation of war—often
very near its reality—was at once a high enjoyment
and a noble accomplishment. It was enacted by
various statutes, commencing with an Act passed in
the Parliament at Winchester, in the thirteenth year
of Edward I., "that every man have harness in his
house to keep the peace after the ancient assize,—that
is to say, every man between fifteen years of age and
sixty years, shall be assessed and sworn to armour according to the quantity of his lands and goods." As
the bow was the favourite weapon of the English pea-
santry, regular practice was enforced, and shooting
was both the training and the amusement of all
whose property in land did not amount to forty shillings in value. Every hamlet had its pair of butts:
and on Sundays and holidays—our ancestors would
have marvelled at the dedication of the Sabbath to
religion, sloth, or drink—all able-bodied men were
required to present themselves in the field, and to
employ their leisure hours "as valyant Englishmen
ought to do." Mayors, bailiffs, and headboroughs
were directed to see these manly amusements observed; and if they neglected to do so, were fined twenty

shillings for each proven omission of their duty. It is interesting to remark how sedulously our legislators five centuries ago discouraged "unthrifty games," and especially such as, being of a sedentary kind, might be practised in taverns and places of ill-resort. Numerous are the statutes levelled by the Parliaments of the Plantagenets against "the plays of bowls, quoits, dice, kails;" as numerous the complaints of veteran soldiers against the addiction of the younger sort of recruits to dancing, carding, and dicing! Many of the national sports indeed have justly fallen into comparative desuetude, and we now seldom read of bull-baitings or prize-fights. With these and with all amusements that involve cruelty to animals, or brutalize those who practise them, we can well dispense; yet we may be allowed to regret the abeyance of foot-ball on the village camping land, and the periodical matches of wrestlers at wakes and fairs. It is one of the highest recommendations of cricket that it brings together men of all degrees; and we quite go with Lord John Manners in his benevolent wish to devise and promote all such recreations as equalize ranks, and wherein superior skill is the only distinction. The benefits of such equalization were proved in the wars of Edward III. It is observed by the contemporary chronicles, that one cause of the higher courage and more effective discipline of the English at Crecy and Poitiers was attributable to the terms on which the chivalry of England lived with its yeomanry. In the French armies, the archers and light troops were held aloof by the knights and their squires as a rabble, good only for the prelude to the fight, but infinitely beneath the rank or notice of the men-at-arms. Whereas in the English host a common cordiality and a generous emulation pervaded all the ranks; the serried line of the archers had its place and consideration as well as the mounted columns of horse, were taken into account by the commissariat, and scrupulously tended in the hospital. The effects of this cohesion were felt long after the bow was forgotten as a weapon of offence; and it is in some measure owing to the more comprehensive character of our national amusements, that amid our acrimonious political contests and even occasional revolutions, there has never been such a severance of classes as hastened the downfall of the commonwealth of Rome and the monarchy of France.

In the sixteenth and seventeenth centuries, masques and plays constituted a prominent feature in the pastimes of the English people. The world has hitherto seen three great dramatic eras in three distinct nations; and the eminence of Greece, Spain, and England, in this province of art, may be attributed to the intense sympathy of their population generally with dramatic passion and pageantry. Of Greece and Spain it must suffice to observe, that their great dramatic eras correspond nearly with the most vigorous development of the national energies. Greece owed to the fusion of classes, resulting from her invasion by Persia and to the national exultation consequent on its conclusion, all the nobler and most vital elements of her dramatic literature. The restless activity which propelled Spain in the fifteenth century towards enterprise in Europe and the New World, broke down in some degree her provincial differences and isolation, and fused into one mass the conflicting and diversified elements of her people. Her theatre was the exponent of the national triumphs, and reflected to her, in the noblest mirrors of poetry, the deeds and sufferings that had rendered her great. Her dramatic literature indeed was the only point at which the upper and lower classes of the Spanish people really osculated. The Court and the nobles were too deeply entrenched behind their own pride and immunities to blend readily with the middle orders; the towns were sharply distinguished from the country; the inland provinces, where the people were shepherds or vine-growers, from the coast provinces, where the inhabitants were engrossed by either regular or irregular trade. In the Spanish drama however there existed a common point of union for all these classes, and it exhibits the characteristics of the nation even more fully than the popular spectacles. The English drama rests upon a broader basis than that of either Athens or Madrid. The avenues to it had been prepared in the ruder periods of the Plantagenets. For not only were masques and plays acted at Court, or in the castles of the nobles, but itinerant companies wandered, as in ancient Greece, from village to village, performing in barns or taverns, or in the farmhouse kitchen, Moralities and Mysteries—the preludial notes of Marlowe and Shakespeare. To ourselves, who can measure the effect of such rude foreshadowings only by the impression they would now produce, these legends, in which saints and angels are actors, and the Deity himself often an interlocutor, wear the semblance of profanity. Yet it is a semblance only, for they were believed when represented, were conceived in good faith, and were acted with devout earnestness. They were no more profane than the early quaintnesses of painting, or the subtle investigations of the schoolmen. They were the expressions of an imaginative age upon subjects which reject the cold conclusions of the reason. They were, moreover, at a time when few could read and fewer write, the alphabet of a people who felt strongly even if they understood darkly; and to the passionate emotions occasionally displayed in the "Moralities" we owe much of the loftier and more eloquent passion of the national drama. All great nations are indeed dramatic, because life is at one period of their fortunes a simple phenomenon and an overpowering mystery. They see in part, and they prophesy in part; and both their vision and their apprehensions are in earnest. To produce a great dramatist, the drama must previously be the passion

N

of a people. The drama in the sixteenth century was the especial amusement of the English from the palace to the village-green. The English were then in a similar condition to the Athenians at the epoch of their invasion by Persia. They felt strong in themselves and in their power over circumstances. They had survived wars that drained the nation's best blood; they were troubled neither with social problems, nor subjective speculations; their vigour and spirits were exuberant, and new avenues seemed opening on all sides for their sinewy strength of mind and body. The resources of ancient literature had recently been opened to them; the new products of the Christian mind of Europe were being daily brought within their ken. Their native ballads and legends were still sung or recited in streets, markets, and by firesides; and their fancy was stimulated by the revelation of lands beyond what had been long supposed to be a trackless and impassable ocean. Under this combination of emotions and circumstahces, the English drama began to erect the steps of that august throne which Shakespeare was destined to occupy.

Hereafter we may return to the subject of Popular Amusements. We have surveyed the subject briefly under various phases—some at the culmination, others at the commencement of their growth. But a field far beyond our present limits remains to be explored; and we can at present only find room for a few brief remarks on the importance of national pastimes to all who study the past or speculate upon the future history of the civilized world.

A trivial and inexpressive portion only of national life is reflected in the public acts of a people. We may comprehend the tissue of its wars and negotiations, its commerce, arts, and manufactures, without therefore apprehending its passions and prejudices, or the general *clinamen* of its temper. What it does spontaneously is the emblem and exponent of its interior being; and since amusements cannot be enforced and must be spontaneous, it is worth the while of historians to read the public history of a nation by the light of its recreations. No less incumbent is it on the legislators, for the present and the future, to study the undisguised aspect of the people for whom it legislates. Charles and Laud might have saved their own heads, and the removal of a throne and hierarchy to boot, had they condescended to survey calmly the physiognomy of England in their days. Not a small blunder might recently have been shunned, if the true significance of the cry for " Sunday recreations" had been more subtly scrutinized. It is a question that should have been treated on its broadest ground or left undisturbed. Well were it, too, for the Church, and for every denomination which has intentionally or inadvertently supported her on this question, to ponder whither they are wending by their opposition to a just demand, or by their partial compliance with a senseless clamour. If not determined now, it must at least very soon be mooted and decided, whether Governments shall deal only with the hard and repulsive elements of social policy, or whether they shall extend their cares and studies to the more spontaneous and genial desires of the community. The State is no less a parent than a schoolmaster; and while it necessarily provides penalties for the erring members of its household, it should with equal vigilance and sympathy afford space and verge enough for the recreations which may divert the masses from sensual indulgence and specious temptations, and diffuse a relish for exercises and pastimes that promote at once health of body and cheer and content of spirit.

THE END.

JOHN EDWARD TAYLOR, PRINTER,
LITTLE QUEEN STREET, LINCOLN'S INN FIELDS.